W9-ATY-079

TSUBASA

THOSE WITH WINGS

8-2018
AFC
549
941373

By Natsuki Takaya

TOKYOPOP®

HAMBURG // LONDON // LOS ANGELES // TOKYO

Tsubasa: Those with Wings Volume 1

Story and Art by Natsuki Takaya

Translation - Kinami Watabe
English Adaptation - Stephanie Duchin
Retouch and Lettering - Star Print Brokers
Production Artist - Michael Paolilli
Graphic Designer - Louis Csontos

Editor - Alexis Kirsch
Pre-Production Supervisor - Vicente Rivera, Jr.
Pre-Production Specialist - Lucas Rivera
Managing Editor - Vy Nguyen
Senior Designer - Louis Csontos
Senior Designer - James Lee
Senior Editor - Bryce P. Coleman
Senior Editor - Jenna Winterberg
Associate Publisher - Marco F. Pavia
President and C.O.O. - John Parker
C.E.O. and Chief Creative Officer - Stu Levy

A TOKYOPOP® Manga

TOKYOPOP and are trademarks or registered trademarks of TOKYOPOP Inc.

TOKYOPOP Inc.
5900 Wilshire Blvd. Suite 2000
Los Angeles, CA 90036

E-mail: info@TOKYOPOP.com
Come visit us online at www.TOKYOPOP.com

TSUBASA WO MOTSU MONO by Natsuki Takaya Natsuki Takaya 1995 All rights reserved. First published in Japan in 2007 by HAKUSENSHA, INC., Tokyo English language translation rights in the United States of America and Canada arranged with HAKUSENSHA, INC., Tokyo through Tuttle-Mori Agency Inc., Tokyo English text copyright © 2009 TOKYOPOP Inc.

All rights reserved. No portion of this book may be reproduced or transmitted in any form or by any means without written permission from the copyright holders. This manga is a work of fiction. Any resemblance to actual events or locales or persons, living or dead, is entirely coincidental.

ISBN: 978-1-4278-1428-9

First TOKYOPOP printing: March 2009

10 9 8 7 6 5 4 3 2

Printed in the USA

CONTENTS

Tsubasa: Those With Wings Volume 1

Tsubasa: Those With Wings ---------- 5

Tsubasa: Those With Wings Video Letter ---------- 367

ザ
ッ

翼を持つ者
つばさ
もの
Tsubasa: Those With Wings

Ah, hello...
WELCOME TO OUR STORY OF A WORLD OF LOVE AND LUST.
Nooo!
IT'S A LIE! HE'S A BIG FAT LIAR!!
Anyhow, here we go...

WE ARE IN THE 22ND CENTURY.
THE EARTH IS IN A STATE OF DESOLATION.
THIEF!!
THERE WERE SO MANY WARS...
THE FIELDS ARE WITHERED AND BUILDINGS LAY IN RUIN.
THE ONLY ONES WHO HAVE ACCESS TO THE NICER AMENITIES NOW ARE THE RICH, THE ARMY, AND THE POLITICIANS.
MEANWHILE, ORDINARY PEOPLE SUFFER IN POVERTY.

THUD
Ow.
IT'S THE THIEF KOTOBUKI!
WHOA.
Damn!!
JUMPING AROUND, AS USUAL.
SHE'S A MONKEY!!
GYAAAAH!!
すげ
ざざざざ
DAMMIT!
I HATE IT WHEN THEY CALL ME A MONKEY!
YOU GO AROUND THE BACK--
WHERE'S THE CAPTAIN?!
HE'S GOING SOLO AGAIN.

IT'S BEEN SIX MONTHS, I THINK.
YOU STEAL ANYTHING GOOD?
Go away!!
YOU'RE AN OFFICER IN THE ARMY!
DON'T YOU HAVE WORK TO DO?!
IF I FELT LIKE IT...
...I COULD CATCH YOU IN A MATTER OF SECONDS.
KOTOBUKI?
RAAAIMON...
MY BAD. YOU OKAY?
THAT'S SO MEAN...
ALL YOU DO IS JUMP AROUND LIKE A LITTLE MONKEY.
YOU NEVER STEAL ANYTHING OF VALUE.
BUT YOU'R NOT REALL WORTH IT

HE MAKES ME SO MAD.
HE'S IRRESPONSIBLE AND MEAN AS EVER!!
I BET IT WON'T BE LONG BEFORE THEY GET TIRED OF YOU BEING A LOSER!!
.....
I'M DOING YOU A FAVOR.
...AND YOU NEVER ARRESTED ME BECAUSE...?
SO IT'S BEEN TWO AND A HALF YEARS...
BASTARD!!
Oh, yeah?
GEE, THANKS!
YOU REALLY WANT TO BET ON THAT?
EH?!
AND IF YOU LOSE...
I'LL GET YOU NEXT TIME.
RUN FOR YOUR LIFE.

ONE MINUTE YOU'RE SOUND ASLEEP, AND THE NEXT--
Oh!
YOU SCARED ME, KOTOBUKI.
No way, Raimon! I'll never take that bet!
Geez...
...ABOUT SOMETHING THAT HAPPENED THREE MONTHS AGO...
I HAD A BAD DREAM...
OH...
I HAD NO MONEY, NO PLACE TO STAY.
MY LIFE WAS QUITE MISERABLE.
I'VE MADE A LIVING AS A THIEF SINCE I WAS SIX.
I DID WHAT I HAD TO DO TO SURVIVE.
RIGHT... IT WAS ONLY THREE MONTHS AGO.
WE SHOULD GET GOING. BREAK TIME IS ALMOST OVER.
AW...
B-but...!

I FOUND MY FIRST JOB IN THIS TOWN...
じゅーん
KOTOBUKI!?
FIN-ALLY...
I'VE BEEN WAITING FOR THIS DAY FOR 16 YEARS...!!
ON THE DOUBLE, KOTOBUKI!!
HURRY UP AND BRING IN SOME FIREWOOD!!
I GOT IT, OKAY?!!
THE BOSS IS MEAN AND THE WORK IS HARD, BUT...
へっぽ
へっぽ
KOTOBUKI, GO GET PLATES FROM THE BACK.
AND THE ROOF NEEDS REPAIRING!!
GOT IT.
HE'S GOING TO BOSS YOU AROUND...
...UNTIL YOU DROP, KOTOBUKI.
It's fine!
IT'S MY JOB TO DO ALL THAT.
IT FEELS A LOT BETTER THAN ROBBING PEOPLE.

OUCH!
WATCH YOUR HAND, OLD MAN!
I almost broke some plates!!
WHO DO YOU THINK YOU'RE TALKING TO?
I'M A WANDERER! MY JOURNEY JUST TOOK ME TO THIS TOWN!
HOLD ON A SEC! I DIDN'T RUN AWAY FROM HIM!!
Heh...
AND I'M FAR AWAY FROM RAIMON.
HE'D NEVER COME THIS FAR OUT.
WHOA!
WHERE'S MY FOOD, YOU SLACKER?!
THANKS.
KOTOBUKI?
GEEZ. HE THINKS THAT JUST BECAUSE HE'S THE WEALTHIEST MAN IN TOWN, HE HAS THE RIGHT TO TREAT US LIKE DIRT.
I CAN TAKE CARE OF THE PLATES, KOTOBUKI.
KOTOBUKI!
Tsk!
YOU'D BETTER BE, YOU SCUM!
...I'M SORRY ABOUT THAT...

?!
OOF.
THE THIEF KOTOBUKI?
...I'LL TAKE THAT AS A YES.
MY NAME IS SHOKA. IT'S NICE TO MEET YOU.
RELAX. WE'RE COL-LEAGUES.
MAY I HAVE A WORD WITH YOU?
...IT'S JUST THAT ROBBING IS NOT MY CALLING.
ANYWAY, WHAT DO OU WANT?!
WHY ARE YOU WORKING AS A WAITRESS, KOTOBUKI?

HELP US FIND TSUBASA.
YOU'RE NOT MUCH OF A THIEF, BUT YOU'VE GOT SPEED. AND THAT'S A GREAT ASSET.
WHY DON'T YOU COME JOIN US? DON'T GET STUCK HERE.
I'VE HEARD ABOUT YOU.
A GIRL AROUND 15 OR 16, WHO IS VERY NIMBLE...
...LIKE A MONKEY.
WHY DO THEY ALWAYS SAY THAT?!
Damn!!
ONCE UPON A TIME, THERE WAS A SMALL, POOR TOWN.
AND ONE DAY, FROM BELOW THE GROUND...
YOU'RE ACTUALLY LOOKING FOR IT?
TSUBASA... YOU MEAN THE TSUBASA?
THAT'S RIGHT. THE LEGENDARY TSUBASA.
THERE'S A MYTH...
RUMOR HAS IT THAT THE ARMY'S SECRETLY AFTER IT, TOO.
WELL, WE'RE NOT THE ONLY ONES. THERE'RE LOTS OF PEOPLE OUT THERE LOOKING FOR IT.

SOME PEOPLE BELIEVE THAT IT STILL LAYS SOMEWHERE DEEP IN THE GROUND, AND THAT WHOEVER FINDS IT...
...WILL GET HIS WISH...
...SORRY ABOUT THAT.
I'VE GOT A JOB, SO I'M NOT INTERESTED.
YOU BETTER NOT UNDERPLAY OUR BOSS.
GRR...
Well, damn
YOU CAN DROP THE TOUGH GIRL ACT, YOU STUPID CHILD.
SEE YOU LATER.
WHAT DID YOU SAY?!!
THIS ISN'T OVER. YOU HAVEN'T SEEN THE LAST OF US, HONEY.
...TSUBASA EMERGED, SHOOTING OFF THOUSANDS OF LIGHTS...
...AND IT VANISHED AFTER GRANTING EACH OF THE VILLAGERS' WISHES.
SOME BECAME RICH, WHILE SOME GAINED ETERNAL LIFE.
WHAT IT LOOKS LIKE, HOW ONE MAKES IT APPEAR, OR WHY IT IS CALLED TSUBASA REMAINS A MYSTERY, BUT...

"DROP THE TOUGH GIRL ACT."
HOW DARE SHE!
I'VE ALWAYS BEEN ON MY OWN.
I NEVER THOUGHT THAT SOME PEOPLE ACTUALLY BELIEVED IN IT...
SHE CAN BE A REAL BITCH, AND SHE CAN'T RUN AND HAS TERRIBLE AIM.
DON'T SAY ANOTHER WORD!!
I'll hit you!!
UH, OKAY...
EVERY DAY, I'VE BEEN THE ONLY ONE I COULD RELY ON...
...BECAUSE THERE WAS NO ONE TO TURN TO.
Shit.
BOSS?!
TSUBASA GRANTS EVERYONE'S WISHES...
TSU BASA
ぶんぶんぶんぶん
STOP IT. I'VE GOT WORK TO DO!!
GO AWAY I DON'T WANT YOU
I'M ON IT, SIR...
KOTOBUKI.

RAIMON?!
UH.
R--
HEY.
LONG TIME NO SEE.
HE'S EAL!!
I'M ON VACATION.
B-BUT WHY RE YOU OUT IN HE MIDDLE OF NOWHERE...?!
OTOBUKI.
BUT... WHY?
Y-YOU...
WHAT'RE YOU DOING...?
WHAT AM I SAYING?!

SO I GOT A GLIMPSE.
YOU COULD'VE CLOSED YOUR EYES!!
What are you, crazy?!!
I DIDN'T KNOW YOU WORE A GIRDLE. THAT'S FRAUD.
GASP!
DID...
DID YOU REALLY MEAN IT...?
UH, ABOUT THAT BET...
Heh...
I KNEW IT.
I SHOULDN'T HAVE TAKEN YOU SERIOUSLY, BUT...
...RIGHT.
BET?
WHAT BET?

Morning grocery shopping

I OVERHEARD THE TWO OF YOU YELLING YESTERDAY. YOU KNOW EACH OTHER?

I'M SO GLAD I DIDN'T SAY ANYTHING ABOUT BEING A THIEF...

WELL, A BIT...

THAT RAIMON GUY THAT'S STAYING HERE. IS HE IN THE ARMY?

HOW DID YOU KNOW?!

Is that so?

THAT'S THEIR JOB, AFTER ALL. RAIMON'S AN EXCEPTION...

I'VE SEEN SOME OFFICERS IN TOWN, BUT THEY ALL LOOK SCARY.

GOOD FOR YOU. KNOWING SOMEONE FROM THE ARMY.

すぱっ

YOU KNOW, THAT RAIMON IS SO COOL! ♡ COULD YOU ASK IF HE HAS A GIRLFRIEND?

No...

NOT A CHANCE!!

DO YOU THINK HE'S ONE OF THE ARMY'S ELITE?

I HEARD THAT IF YOU WORK YOUR WAY UP TO CAPTAIN, YOU'RE REWARDED WITH A HOUSE WITH ELECTRICITY AND RUNNING WATER!!

Money and glory... The elite have it all.

HE'S AN IRRESPONSIBLE AND MANIPULATIVE JERK.
ふはは
はは
HE THINKS IT'S ALL A BIG JOKE!!
Wait...
KOTOBUKI?
HE'S BEEN LIKE THAT EVER SINCE WE MET.
BECAUSE...
.....
THAT'S RIGHT. WHY WOULD I WANT TO ASK HIM THAT?
Ha!
WHAT A JOKE.
HE'D THINK I WAS INTERESTED IN HIM!!
YOU KNOW!!
HE MIGHT GET A FUNNY IDEA.
"NICE TO MEET YOU."
"ARE YOU KOTOBUKI? YOU'RE CUTE."
THAT'D BE DIS-GUSTING!
"AND YOU'RE AN IDIOT. DO YOUR JOB."
"I WILL..."
"...EVENTUALLY."
KYAA!!

HUH...?
A LETTER?
Old-fashioned--
ARE YOU GOING TO READ IT...?
Gasp!

..."KOTOBUKI IS BAD NEWS. FIRE HER OR SOMETHING BAD WILL HAPPEN..."
WH--
THAT'S AWFUL.

...TOOOBUUUK!!!??
Boss
GAH!

IT MUST BE THAT WOMAN...
SHOKA!!
KO...
How im-mature.

Explain! Now!
What hav you done this time?
Wait--
HOLD ON A SEC, BOSS!!
.....

AH!
I DON'T WANT ANY TROUBLE. BEAT IT!!
HOLD ON A SEC! YOU HAVEN'T PAID ME YET!
SHUT UP AND LEAVE!
A-AND I DIDN'T GET TO EAT MY BREAKFAST, AND...
Shut up!!
HOW MUCH DO YOU THINK GLASS COSTS NOWADAYS?
DEDUCT IT FROM MY SALARY!!
JUST DON'T DO THIS TO ME!!
BUT I SUPPOSE...
THIS...
...I HAD IT COMING.
...IS ONE OF THOSE TIMES...
..WHEN I FEEL LIKE...
DAMN...
NOT AGAIN...
I WORKED SO HARD FOR IT...
ALL I WANTED WAS TO START A NEW, CLEAN LIFE.
...I COULD REALLY USE A BIG SHOULDER TO LEAN ON.

Again
Why did I have to think of him?!
FORGET THAT! SULKING WON'T GET ME ANYWHERE!!
THEY CAN'T GET ME DOWN!!
I GUESS IT'S BACK TO A LIFE OF...
... CRIME.
KEEP YOUR VOICE DOWN, YOU IMBECILE!!
!
THAT'S THE RICH GUY FROM YESTERDAY...
ANYWAY.
THIS IS EXTREMELY VALUABLE.
What?!
IS THAT TRUE, SIR?!!
HOWEVER...
...I'M S HUNGR ...

WHAT'S THAT?
IT'S SOMETHING THE ARMY WOULD KILL TO HAVE.
I CAN'T WAIT TO FIND OUT HOW MUCH THEY'RE WILLING TO PAY FOR IT.
IT'S THE ONLY ONE IN THE WORLD.
WHAT ARE THEY TALKING ABOUT?
"...THE ARMY'S SECRETLY AFTER IT, TOO."
Oh!
COULD BE...
...TSUBASA...?
HM...?
NOT SO LOUD.
NGHHH! NGHHH!
I HEAR YOU GOT FIRED.
ブル
ルルルル
!!
ひぃ
YOU POOR THING...
Get off!
Oh.

YOU'RE SHAKING.
IT'LL BE FINE. I CAN FIND ANOTHER JOB. UNTIL THEN...
...I'LL JUST GET BETTER AT STEALING--
ARE YOU AFRAID?
LISTEN, I'M BACK IN THE GAME AS OF TODAY!!
THEN YOU NEED TO BE A NOTCH UP FROM THAT.
I CAN'T GET COMFY WITH AN OFFICER!
How's that?!
DO YOU EVEN GET THE MEANING OF THAT PHRASE?
I AM A NOTCH UP!
UH.
How'd you know?!
It's obvious.
I DIDN'T KNOW YOU WERE INTERESTED IN TSUBASA--
I-I--
I'M JUST CURIOUS...
That's all...
I...
BREAK IN THAT MAN'S HOUSE?
ANYWAY, I'M GOING TO--
LET GO OF ME, YOU LOSER!!

I'M GOING WITH YOU.
WHA--?
YOU WORK FOR THE LAW ENFORCEMENT, REMEMBER?!
I'M ON VACA-TION.
Idiot!!
THAT DOESN'T MAKE IT OKAY!!
I WON'T STEAL ANYTHING.
I'LL JUST WATCH.
がく
HAVE YOU NO PRIDE AS AN OFFICER?!
?
?!
Oh.
HE'S THE OFFICER IN CHARGE OF THIS SECTOR.
WE'VE GOT TO GO.
Wait.
WHY ARE YOU FOLLOWING ME?
YOU KNOW WHY.
City dweller
POOR CAPTAIN YUGEN, WASTING AWAY IN THE COUNTRYSIDE.
CRUD!
Let's get going.

WHAT DO YOU WANT FROM ME? ARE YOU PULLING MY LEG?
AND...
I CAN'T ASK THAT, THOUGH.
SOON ENOUGH YOU'LL FORGET WHAT YOU JUST SAID, JUST LIKE YOU DID WITH THE BET.
I JUST WANT TO BE WITH YOU, KOTOBUKI.
WHEN DID HE START HAVING THIS EFFECT ON ME?
I'M DANCING TO HIS RHYTHM.
I WISH I KNEW HOW HE FEELS ABOUT ME.
IF ONLY I HAD TSUBASA...
...TSUBASA COULD MAKE THAT HAPPEN.
IF I HAD TSUBASA, I WOULD BE ABLE TO TELL.

LOOKS LIKE OUR LETTER WORKED.
LET'S FOLLOW HER UNTIL SHE GIVES IN AND JOINS US.
SHE'S GOT COMPANY. A GUY...
BOSS.
KOTOBUKI IS ON THE MOVE.
GOT IT.
...SO THIS IS HIS HOUSE.
Okay...
SO HOW ARE WE GOING TO GET IN?
YOU'RE REALLY COMING ALONG?!
Let's go!!
THEN TAKE CARE OF HIM.
DOES SHE EVER WORK...?
DON'T EVEN BOTHER, OR SHE'LL START CHUCKING EXPLOSIVES AT YOU.
She always misses, though.

YOU WANT A QUICK MEAL?
CAN I COME WITH YOU?
"CAN" I?
CAN I?
DO WHAT YOU WANT!!
Yay!
OKAY! LET'S GO.
すくっ

DO YOU MIND IF I GO FIRST?
IF I GO DOWN FROM HERE--
"I DIDN'T KNOW YOU WORE A GIRDLE. THAT'S FRAUD."
BLUSH
NO!! I'LL GO FIRST!!
Final word!!
...OKAY...
MAYBE ...
...I SHOULD'VE CHANGED MY CLOTHES...
WHAT'RE YOU DOING?
Gaaah!
AH.
I DON'T KNOW WHERE TO START...
I THINK WE'VE FOUND SOME-THING.
HM?

James L. Hamner Public Library
Amelia Court House, VA 23002

BUT YOU GOT IT ILLEGALLY, DIDN'T YOU?
Naughty old man.
Shut up!!
YOU'VE SEEN TOO MUCH. I'M AFRAID I'LL HAVE TO KILL BOTH OF YOU.
Aren't you scared?
LIKE...
...THE PLACE WHERE YOU HOLD AUCTIONS?
Ack!
Ah.
SO THAT'S WHAT YOU WERE LOOKING FOR.
IT'S NOT HERE. I HID IT IN A SAFE PLACE.
GIVE US A SEND-OFF GIFT.
WHERE DID YOU STASH "THE ONLY ONE IN THE WORLD"?
HE SAID HE'S GOT CLUES ON TSUBASA IN THIS HOUSE!!
?!
You little--
Hey, don't provoke him. He's got a gun...
YOU'RE TOO DUMB TO MAKE GOOD USE OF IT.
YOU SHOULD WATCH THAT BIG MOUTH OF YOURS.
THEY'RE ALL MINE!
YOU ARE NOT GOING TO TAKE ANYTHING FROM ME.
NOT A PENNY. NOT A THING.

Whaaat?!
GAH!!
WHERE?!
WHERE IS IT?!
YEP.
YOU KNEW SHE WAS FOLLOWING US, DIDN'T YOU?!
HE'S OUT COLD.
WHERE IS IT, KOTO--
Damn-!
HE'S USELESS, THEN.
ずざっ
Ra-
RAIMON?!
You...
YOU TWO KNOW EACH OTHER?!
YEP.
WHAT ARE YOU DOING HERE?
YOU QUIT THE ARMY...
...TWO MONTHS AGO!!

"THEY CAN BLAME ME, AND IT'LL MAKE IT EASIER FOR ME TO QUIT THE ARMY."
"YOU'RE GOING TO ABANDON YOUR STATUS?!"
"THERE IS SOMETHING I WANT TO DO."
NO, WHAT ARE YOU TALKING ABOUT?!
WHAT'RE YOU TALKING ABOUT? HE'S ON VACATION.
Heh.
.....
"I'M GOING TO LET YOU ESCAPE."
I KNOW BECAUSE I WAS THERE!!
...YOU NEVER ARRESTED ME?
BECAUSE THERE WAS SOMETHING ELSE YOU'D RATHER DO...?
"I'LL GET YOU NEXT TIME."
WHY...
DID HE LIE?
IS THAT WHY...
IS THAT TRUE...?
AND JUST LIKE THAT, HE QUIT!!
YEAH.

SO THE BET REALLY WAS JUST A WHIM OF YOURS.
AND YOU FORGOT ALL ABOUT IT.
ANYWAY, I AM EXTREMELY CLOSE TO GETTING TSUBASA.
I'm not afraid of Raimon!
LOOKS LIKE I DON'T NEED YOUR HELP AFTER ALL, KOTOBUKI...
HEY!!
I was still talking!!
TSUBASA...
...IS MINE!
THIS IS TOO MUCH, EVEN FOR TSUBASA.
BOM
BOM
WHOA!
OUCH...
I've got a dirt in my eye...
GEEZ. SHE'S HORRIBL
WHAT SHOULD I DO?
HELP ME, TSUBASA.
GYAAA!
RAIMON...?
WHERE...?

!!
JUST GREAT... YOU ALMOST HAD ME FOOLED, KOTOBUKI.
YOU WANT TSUBASA, TOO, DON'T YOU?
YOU DON'T EVEN HAVE TO WORK FOR IT!
THERE'S NOTHING WRONG WITH THAT. TSUBASA CAN MAKE YOU RICH. NO MORE ROBBING, RIGHT?
IT OPENS DOORS TO EVERYTHING.
DEEP DOWN, EVERYBODY WANTS AN EASY LIFE.
I DON'T KNOW WHAT YOU WERE DOING WORKING STEADY...
...BUT YOU'RE NO DIFFERENT THAN THE OTHERS.
I JUST DIDN'T WANT TO ADMIT IT.
IF I LOST FAITH IN MYSELF, I WOULDN'T BE ABLE TO KEEP GOING.
SHE'S RIGHT.
...MAYBE SHE'S RIGHT.
MAYBE IT WAS POINTLESS TO EVEN TRY.
Wow, boss!! You're a bitch!!!
Shut it!!

I WAS JUST ACTING TOUGH.
NOT ME.
IF I REALLY WANTED SOMETHING...
...I'D WANT TO EARN IT ON MY OWN.
LET'S GO.
.....
げしっ
YOU--
THEN MIND YOUR OWN BUSINESS!!
STOP MESSING WITH KOTOBUKI.
HANG IN THERE, BOSS!!
You look really stupid!!

THIS IS WHERE HE HIDES HIS STASH.
HUH?
CAPTAIN RAIMON?!
IS THAT CAPTAIN RAIMON SHIRAGI?!
OW!
THE POLICE!!
WHAT WAS THAT NOISE?!
OH.
IF YOU DON'T WANT TO GET CAUGHT...
...GO ON WITHOUT ME WHILE I TALK TO HIM.
OH... OKAY.
HUH?
WAIT.
WHAT'S GOING...
...ON?
PLEASE GET IN THE CAR!!
LONG TIME NO SEE, YUGEN.
WE'VE BEEN LOOKING FOR YOU.
IT IS GOOD TO SEE YOU.

YOU DON'T EVEN HAVE TO WORK FOR IT!
"IF I WANTED SOMETHING..."
"NOT ME."
BUT...
TSUBASA CAN GET YOU ANYTHING...
THERE'S NO WAY THEY'RE TAKING HIM BACK...
IS THERE?
"I'D WANT TO EARN IT ON MY OWN."
"GOOD GIRL."

I'M NO GOOD.
I CAN'T DO ANYTHING RIGHT.
WHO'S THAT BRAT? WHAT DOES SHE WANT WITH CAPTAIN SHIRAGI?
And she's on a first-name basis?!
What?
BUT... I'VE BEEN TRYING.
SO...
I HAVE TO ASK HIM WHAT HE REALLY WANTS.
Ack!
I NEED TO FIND OUT FOR MYSELF.
RAIMON!!
WAIT UP!!

EVERYONE HAS HIGH HOPES FOR YOU, RAIMON.
THEY MADE YOU A CAPTAIN AS PART OF THE TRAINING.
YOU HAVE A GREAT CAREER AHEAD OF YOU.
COME BACK WITH US.
STAY WHERE YOU ARE!!
I'VE GOT TO GO FOR IT!!
MIND IF I BORROW THIS?
RAIMON--
LATER!
THERE IS SOMETHING ELSE I WANT TO DO.
DIDN'T I TELL YOU?
RAIMON? WHAT--
!?
WHOA!

IF YOU EARN IT ON YOUR OWN...
Huff
Huff
BUT...
Huff
Huff
Huff
I BET...
Huff
Huff
...SHOKA DOESN'T UNDERSTAND WHAT I'M...
...DOING...
Huff
Huff
RA...
...WHAT YOU GET IS MUCH MORE MEANINGFUL.
Ahhh!
...I DON'T UNDER-STAND YOU.
RAIMON SHIRAGI...
WHAT IS IT YOU REALLY WANT?
HOP ON.
WHA?!

DON'T WORRY.
.....
I WAS COMING BACK TO YOU!
RAIMON, I...
HOLD ON TIGHT.
HUH?
Whaaat?!
WHA ?!
EXCUSE ME.
GAH!
WAI--
STOP--
Ahhhh!!
*Hot

YOU IDIOT!!
FIST
Head
YOU'RE ALWAYS JERKING ME AROUND...
YOU COULD'VE GOTTEN US KILLED!!
...YOU RECKLESS BASTARD...!
I DON'T.
.....
I DON'T REGRET IT.
WE'RE HERE.
I, UH, KIND OF WRECKED THAT, DIDN'T I?
ドルン
ハッ
ドル
ギィ
ドルン
...OF FINDING OUT THAT HE WAS JUST IN IT, TO HAVE SOME FUN.
'D BE LOST, IF THAT WERE TRUE.
I WAS JUST AFRAID...

I COULDN'T SHOW MY FEAR, THOUGH...
...SINCE IT WAS TIME TO FIND OUT THE TRUTH.
OTHERWISE I'D DIE OF RAIMON DISEASE.
KOTOBUKI.
YOU'RE CUTE.
ドタン
!!
バン
バン
バン
...WH--
WHY...?
OH, DON'T CRY.
IT ONLY MAKES ME WANT TO TEASE YOU MORE.
WHY ARE YOU DOING THIS TO ME?

I TOLD YOU.
"YOU REALLY WANT TO BET ON THAT?"
"I'LL GET YOU NEXT TIME."
"AND IF YOU LOSE..."
I'VE LIED TO YOU AND JERKED YOU AROUND...
YOU CAN HATE ME ALL YOU WANT. I'D UNDERSTAND.
I'LL NEVER LET YOU GO.
SORRY, BUT THAT'S ME.
...JUST TO GET YOUR ATTEN-TION.
I WILL MAKE YOU MINE.

YOU LEFT ALL THE GLORY FOR ME?!
YOU CAN'T BE MORE PRECISE.
IS THAT WHAT YOU WANTED TO DO? TO WIN THE BET...?
Th-that's...
BINGO.
But...
YOU SAID YOU'D FORGOTTEN!!
I DIDN'T SAY THAT.
S--
STUPID. I'M SO STUPID.
ALL I WANTED WAS TO END THE WHOLE OFFICER-THIEF THING SO I COULD BE WITH YOU.
RAIMON...
LOOK BEHIND--
THAT'S...
...WHAT MAKES YOU SO IRRESISTIBLE.

Oh!
THIS IS IT. THIS IS HIS STASH.
IT'S SHORTED OUT.
They're in uniforms. Are they Army?
IS THIS THE CLUE TO TSUBASA?
I DON'T THINK SO. THESE ARE IMAGES OF HUMAN BEINGS BEFORE THE 22ND CENTURY.
I'M NOT SURE IF TSUBASA REALLY EXISTS ANYMORE...
NOT MY PROBLEM.
WHAT THE...
We got it wrong?
EH...?
THEY CAN BE QUITE VALUABLE, SINCE MOST REFERENCES WERE BURNED DURING THE WARS.
BUT MAYBE IT DOESN'T HAVE TO BE BLACK AND WHITE.
YOU SEARCH FOR TSUBASA. YOU DREAM ABOUT IT. YOU INVEST IN IT.

YOU NEED SOMETHING TO LIVE FOR...
...ANY DAY.
...YEAH.
ME...
...TOO.
どぉぉぉん
BOOM
!?
HUMANS ARE WEAK.
SHE'S MAKING THINGS EVEN MORE OF A PROBLEM.
Damn you, Raimon!
Please stop that. The building is falling out.
Sho...
SHOKA...?!
THE DOOR IS BLOCKED, AND THERE'S SHOKA, NOW, TOO.
That's your work, isn't it?!
THERE'S A HOLE IN THE WALL!!
んんんん!!

Uwaaa... That is so not comforting!
DON'T WORRY. I'M THE LUCKY ONE.
WE'LL HAVE TO JUMP OFF.
ARE YOU INSANE? LOOK AT THE HEIGHT!!
I-I can't.
THERE YOU ARE, RAIMON!!
OH!
LET'S GO.
THINK BEFORE YOU ACT, YOU IDIOT!!
Gaaah!
I'm gonna die!
WHY? WHY?!
WHY DOES IT HAVE TO BE HIM?
HE'S CRAZY!
UGHH!!
SHOKA'S SPECIAL BOMB!!
Eat this!!

RIGHT...
OH.
Ouch!!
Koff
Koff
YOU KNEW THERE WAS A LAKE?!
MAYBE?
HE GOT ME...
...AGAIN.
I GUESS.

EEK!!
YOU'RE NOT GOING TO LET HER WALK AWAY WITH NOTHING, RIGHT?
AFTER EVERYTHING SHE'S DONE FOR YOU?
I'LL CONSIDER RE-HIRING HER...
So please don't hit me.
Bully...
WHY SHOULD I TRUST HER WITH YOU?
CAPTAIN RAIMON.
SO YOU'RE REALLY NOT COMING BACK?
YOU JUST WATCH.
Damn!
Ah ha ha ha...
I WILL STEAL YOUR HEART AND NEVER LET YOU GO.

KOTOBUKI.
YOUR BOSS ASKED ME TO HAND THIS TO YOU.
HE'D FORGOTTEN ABOUT IT.
...NOW THAT RAIMON'S FOUND HER.
...SHALL DIE...
HE WHO COMES BETWEEN TWO LOVERS...
DON'T YOU KNOW THE OLD SAYING?
WELL, THAT GIRL'S IN FOR A ROUGH RIDE...
Coming from him, it sounds like a real threat.
...AFTER BEING KICKED BY A HORSE.
OH?!
I'M LEAVING.
Like finding another job.
I FEEL AS IF I CAN DO ANYTHING!
WOW!
MY FIRST SALARY.
WOW! WOW!
BUT... RAIMON?!
HUH...?

RAI--!!
NOT.
I GOT YOU THERE, DIDN'T I?
THIS GUY IS--!!
Damn it!!
GO AHEAD AND LEAVE. SEE IF I CARE.
YOU'RE SO CUTE. YOU KNOW THAT, KOTOBUKI?
Shut up, loser!!
I WANT TO GO HOME.
WHERE'S THE CLUE?!
Back to Shoka.

翼を
持つ者

THE END OF THE 22ND CENTURY: EARTH.
THERE WERE SO MANY WARS...
...THAT HAVE SINCE LEFT THE FIELDS WITHERED. ONLY THE UPPER CLASS PEOPLE, LIKE THE ARMY AND POLITICIANS, ENJOY THE NICER AMENITIES.
PEOPLE ARE FORCED TO LIVE IN POVERTY. THE STREETS ARE RIFE WITH CRIMINALS.
Can't.
I CAN'T AFFORD TO HIRE ANYONE IN THESE HARD TIMES.
NOT IN THIS DRIED-UP VILLAGE WHERE CROPS RARELY GROW.
PLEASE, HIRE ME!!
We just sell household supplies.
SOUNDS LIKE YOU'D MAKE AN EXCELLENT THIEF.
Rocks.
LOOK, I CAN CLIMB. I'VE GOT THE SPEED. I'VE GOT THE STRENGTH!!
Look at me!!
I WANT TO WORK!!
I'M KOTOBUKI. I'M A FORMER THIEF WHO'S LOOKING FOR A REAL JOB.
Wh--
WHAT ARE YOU TALKING ABOUT? WHY WOULD I DO THAT?!

THANKS FOR WAITING, RAIMON.
HUH?!
Where'd he go?!
わぁ…
AND THAT COMPANION...
HOW COME NOBODY WANTS ME...?
キョロ…
...TO SURVIVE THE HARD TIMES.
I USED TO BE A FULL-TIME THIEF. I WAS DOING WHAT I HAD TO DO...
ガヤ
ONE MONTH AGO, I GAINED A COMPANION.
I'VE BEEN TRAVELING FROM TOWN TO TOWN.
ガヤ
JUST GREAT.
...IS HIM.
Ra-
RAI... MON?!
YOU WIN AGAIN.
WHAT THE HECK IS HE DOING?!
ジャラ
ジャラ
MAH-JONG. YOU KNOW HIM? HE'S PRETTY DAMN GOOD.

ゴバッ
ガミ
The table...
HOW DARE YOU BRING ME DOWN TO YOUR LEVEL?
THAT IS AN INSULT.
HE'S CHEATING...
THIS GAME IS RIGGED!
ガタッ
YOU MADE A KILLING, BUDDY.
Can I pick your brain?
OH, IT'S YOU, KOTOBUKI.
I CAN'T BELIEVE HE USED TO BE AN ELITE CAPTAIN IN THE ARMY.
What an odd world.
sigh
RAIMON SHIRAGI: A MEAN AND MANIPULATIVE JERK.
Didn't you know that?
I'M A GENIUS. THERE'S NO BETTER WORD TO DESCRIBE ME.

And you're itching for a beating.
HEY, DID YOU HEAR?
THAT MAN WAS SO MEAN. HE CALLED ME A FAKE.
HOW DID JOB HUNTING GO?
SORRY I KEPT YOU WAITING, BUT CAN'T YOU JUST ACT NORMAL?
ONE DAY HE JUST SHOWED UP AND...
Yo.
RAIMON WOULD CHASE AFTER ME IN HIS OWN FUSSY WAY WHEN I WAS A THIEF.
Wanna chocolate, Kotobuki?
(She's in the middle of a robbery.)
That man scared me out of my wits.
GET. OFF.
THE ARMY IS THE PLACE FOR THE PRIVILEGED FEW.
Damn. He's got company.
Her boys
What?
AFTER A BIT OF FIGHT WITH A FEMALE THIEF CALLED SHOKA...
WORD HAS IT RAIMON WAS A YOUNG CAPTAIN FAST ON TRACK IN THE FORCE. (THIS MAY SOUND UNBELIEVABLE.)
He's out of it.
"ALL I WANTED..."
...I FOUND OUT THAT RAIMON LEFT THE ARMY.
Tsubasa Memo
The force Raimon belonged to is something like the police.

WHAT'S THE MATTER? YOU'RE NOT HUNGRY?
AND HERE WE ARE.
"...WAS TO END THE WHOLE OFFICER-THIEF THING SO I COULD BE WITH YOU."
I SUPPOSE YOU HAD NO LUCK JOB HUNTING.
We--
WE KIND OF LOOK LIKE A COUPLE...!
SO WHY HAVEN'T I HAD ANY LUCK SO FAR?
"Suppose" my ass.
WE'RE TRAVELING FROM TOWN TO TOWN LOOKING FOR A JOB.
No way!!
I'VE GOT A LIST OF THINGS YOU HAVE PAID FOR ME!!
THOSE ARE ALL SELF-IMPOSED DEBTS...
DON'T WORRY. I'M MAKING MONEY.
No!

THE SARABINA TSUBASA CULT.
WHAT'S GOING ON?
IT'S SARABINA.
WHY ARE YOU SO UPSET?
Ngh.
COME ON, THERE'RE NO SECRETS BETWEEN US.
Gaaah
I WISH THERE WAS A JOB LAYING AROUND FOR ME TO PICK UP!!
TSUBASA IS A MYTH OF THIS TIME.
TSUBASA... CULT?
IT GRANTED EVERY VILLAGER'S WISH AND THEN DISAPPEARED INTO THIN AIR.
ONCE UPON A TIME... TSUBASA EMERGED FROM THE GROUND, SHOOTING OFF LIGHTS.

THE PLANET DOES NOT HAVE THE ABILITY TO EXPRESS HER PAIN LIKE US. SHE HAS TO SUFFER IN SILENCE.
AS YOU'RE AWARE...
...THE FIELDS... THE EARTH IS WITHERED.
NOBODY KNOWS WHAT IT LOOKS LIKE, OR WHERE IT CAME FROM.
BUT SOME PEOPLE BELIEVE THAT TSUBASA IS STILL SOMEWHERE DEEP IN THE GROUND...
TSUBASA IS OUR ONLY HOPE.
THE DEATH OF THE EARTH... IS THE DEATH OF US.
WE NEED ITS ABSOLUTE POWER TO SAVE THE PLANET.
...AND THAT WHOEVER FINDS IT WILL BE GRANTED HIS WISH...
TSUBASA WILL DESCEND ONTO THE EARTH ONCE AGAIN AND SAVE US ALL.
NOW WE MAY BE POWERLESS ON OUR OWN...
...BUT IF WE STICK TOGETHER AND PRAY FOR THE LOVE OF TSUBASA...
THAT IS OUR PRAYER, SARABINA'S BELIEF.

わぁ
パチ
パチ
パチ
Kotobuki, want another nikuman?
Uh-huh.
...I'VE HEARD OF SEVERAL TSUBASA CULTS...
...BUT I'VE NEVER HEARD OF SARABINA.
Editor's note: Nikuman a steamed meat bun
IT'S NOT THAT I DON'T BELIEVE IN TSUBASA, BUT...
Cults aren't my thing...
OF COURSE YOU HAVEN'T. THE CULT IS ONLY SIX MONTHS OLD. THEY BUILT A TOWER NEAR THE VILLAGE.
YOU DON'T LOOK FAMILIAR.
Half the village doesn't believe it.
THE WHOLE BUSINESS ABOUT TSUBASA IS BOGUS.
THAT GUY, DUMA, IS THE HEAD. HE GOES AROUND PREACHING PRETTY MUCH EVERY DAY.
ERM...
IF YOU'RE INTERESTED, YOU ARE ALWAYS WELCOME TO VISIT...
...OUR TOWER.
ARE YOU A VISITOR?
OH!

MASTER DUMA...
AH. I MUST GO.
YOU HAVE BAD TASTE.
IT'S SARABINA'S SYMBOL TOWER.
RAIMON!!
WHAT... IS THAT?
THOSE REVOLVING THINGS...
A SYMBOL TOWER... HOW INTER-ESTING.
PRETTY GUY, BUT THERE'S SOMETHING WEIRD ABOUT HIM...
LET THE HAND OF TSUBASA TOUCH UPON YOU...
OKAY...

That' righ!
Heh.
DON'T LET THAT SMILE OF HIS FOOL YOU. YOU NEVER KNOW WHAT'S REALLY GOING ON IN HIS HEAD.
AND WHY DOES THAT ONLY REMIND ME OF YOU?
SIR... ABOUT THAT MAN. HE WAS BEING CALLED RAIMON...
I HEARD...
WELL, WELL... THIS IS A NICE SURPRISE.
WE HAVE TO PREPARE FOR OUR SPECIAL GUESTS.

OR WE COULD JOIN SARABINA AND PRAY FOR TSUBASA.
DON'T EVEN GO THERE.
SO...
DO YOU WANT TO KEEP LOOKING FOR A JOB HERE, OR ARE WE GOING TO THE NEXT TOWN?
Hmm...
LET'S SEE. PEOPLE HERE SEEM TO BE BARELY FEEDING THEMSELVES...
I LIKE TO LOOK AFTER MYSELF...
WHAT IS IT?
Camping
WHAT'S THAT? ON YOUR CHEST...
Right...
THE SIGHT OF IT REMINDS ME THAT YOU WERE AN OFFICER.
SO NO MORE ROBBING? WAS IT A CLEAN BREAK?
THIS? IT'S A TATTOO.
THEY MADE ME GET ONE WHEN I ENTERED THE ARMY.
OF COURSE!! WHAT DO YOU MEAN?!
GRR
DO YOU HAVE A PROBLEM WITH THAT?

TEMPER, TEMPER.
...STILL LOVE YOU NO MATTER WHAT.
I DIDN'T MEAN IT THAT WAY, OKAY?
HUH?
I WILL...
RA--
N--
BUT DON'T WALK AWAY FROM ME, OKAY?
WAIT--
...WE'LL BE ABLE TO SHARE A BED.
WHEN YOU STOP FREAKING OUT OVER A KISS...
I'M SLEEPY AND IT ACHES, I MEAN, MY HEAD, BECAUSE OF A HEADACHE!!
No, stop !!
That was redundant!

DO YOU WANT TO STAY AS A GOOD-FOR-NOTHING?
OF COURSE NOT!!
ギャノ
FIRST THING'S FIRST, I NEED TO FIND SOME WORK...
YEAH, EVERYTHING IS HUNKY-DORY...
WHAT ABOUT ME?
I WAS A THIEF, BUT THAT'S ALL BEHIND ME.
I CAN'T LET RAIMON SEE ME...
...USE STOLEN MONEY. IT'S EMBARRASSING.
Keep dreaming, loser!!
GOOD NIGHT.
パタ
...AWW.
DAMMIT...
WE'VE BEEN TRAVELING TOGETHER FOR A MONTH.
IT'S LONG ENOUGH FOR ME TO KNOW HIS COMPETENCE.
HE'S CAPABLE AND SMART. THERE'S NOTHING HE CAN'T DO.

KOTOBUKI, WHAT TIME DO YOU WANT TO WAKE UP TOMORROW...?
OOPS. SORRY!
Got an eyeful.
.....
.....
GO ROT IN HELL!!

BOSS...
Hell...
Hell...

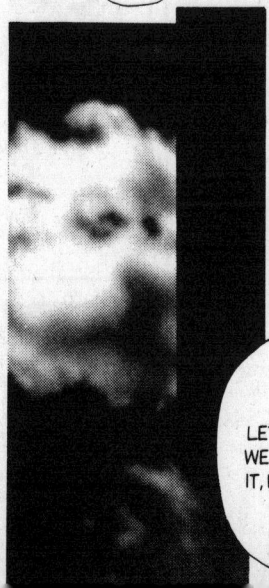

YOU MUST BE IMAGING IT.
THAT ECHOING VOICE SOUNDED FAMILIAR.
LET'S PRETEND WE DIDN'T HEAR IT, RIGHT, BOSS?

I'LL GO CHECK ON RAIMON AGAIN...
I BET HE'S STILL PLAYING MAH-JONG!
NOBODY WANTS ME...
JOB, EH? GOT ONE FOR ME, TOO?!
YOU HAVE TO GO SOME-WHERE ELSE.
SORRY.
HM?
I HAVE AN IDEA.
WHAT'S UP, KIDDO?
Did you drop something?
THERE'RE NO BUDS...
Whee!
Yay!
MAYBE TSUBASA IS THE ONLY ANSWER...
WE WORK ON THE FIELDS EVERY YEAR, BUT THERE'S NO SIGN OF THEM.

KOTOBUKI.
I THOUGHT YOU WERE LOOKING FOR A JOB.
Yay!
Yay!
WHAT DO YOU THINK OF THIS SOIL?
IT'S WONDERFUL!
Thanks, lady!
YEAH, BUT...
WOW, YOU GAVE IT QUITE A WORK-OVER.
YOU HUNGRY?
HMM...
...THAT'S GOOD.
THERE'S STILL GOOD SOIL IF WE KEEP DIGGING.
It's a lot of work, though.

WHY...?
WHY DO WE KEEP BUMPING EACH OTHER?!
Waaaaaah
HE GOT ON HER BAD SIDE...
SHOKA?!
KOTOBUKI ...
...AND RAIMON!!
Who's Who: Shoka
Occupation: Thief who handles explosives. She's set her sights on Tsubasa. She's a slow runner and has terrible aim. She blames Raimon for her bad luck. Poor woman, life hasn't been kind to her.
Relationship: Totally available. She's currently looking for a rich gentleman.
That devil is going to ruin everything for me again!?
Waaah!
SHUT UP!!
I'M NOT TELLING YOU GUYS ANYTHING! YOU WONT GET THE BEST OF US ANYMORE!
LOOKING FOR TSUBASA STILL? WHERE ARE YOU HEADED THIS TIME?
LET'S BE CLEAR ON THIS. IT WASN'T MY FAULT.
WE'RE READY TO GO TO SARABINA TO LOOK FOR CLUES TO TSUBASA WHEN YOU ARE.
Uh. Oops.

OKAY.
DUMA KURY. HE COMES FROM OLD MONEY.
HE SET UP THE SARABINA CULT SIX MONTHS AGO. THEY HAVE 30 FOLLOWERS SO FAR.
...AND THAT SYMBOL TOWER OF HIS. IT'S A WIND POWER STATION, ISN'T IT?
WHAT IS THAT?
YES, THAT'S RIGHT.
THAT REVOLVING THING IS AN ELECTRICITY GENERATING SYSTEM.
A PRIVATE ELECTRIC GENERATOR IS NOT ILLEGAL. WHY HIDE IT...?
Wind-driven power!
WHAT?!
THAT'S INCREDIBLE.
THE GENERATED ELECTRICITY RUNS DOWN TO THE BASEMENT.
WE GOT A THERMAL RESPONSE. THEY HAVE SOMETHING IN THE BASEMENT.
YOU'RE A JERK, AND YOU ALWAYS HAVE BEEN.
WAIT, ARE YOU INTERESTED IN IT BECAUSE IT'S CALLED "TSUBASA" CULT?
Please tell me you're not that naive.

I'M NOT STANDING IN YOUR WAY.
Shoot!!
I'VE TOLD YOU EVERYTHING. NOW, BEAT IT.
GET OUT OF HERE, AND DON'T STAND IN MY WAY.
I'M JUST STEPPING ON YOU BECAUSE YOU'RE IN MY WAY.
And...
BOSS SAID IT'S NOT JUST AN ORDINARY TOWER. HER THIEF'S INSTINCT TOLD HER THAT...
YOU REALLY HAVE A BIG MOUTH.
ow...
Welcome
Lunch & Dinner
...HEY...
WHAT DO YOU THINK SARABINA'S DOING, RUNNING ELECTRICITY IN THE BASEMENT?
NO IDEA. I DON'T WANT TO GET INVOLVED.
GOOD DAY.
GO TO HELL....

RIGHT?
WHA?!
It's him!
IT'S NICE TO SEE YOU AGAIN.
OKAY...
Why are you here?
YOU TWO MAKE A CUTE COUPLE.
YOU'RE A LOVELY YOUNG LADY...
!!
GET OFF, YOU TRANNIE!!
MASTER DUMA!!

...DOES YOUR LESSON INCLUDE WOOING WOMEN?
WHAT AM I SAYING?
ドカ
ドカ
ドカ
I DON'T...
I DON'T LET...
...ANYONE BUT RAIMON TOUCH ME!!
IF IT WEREN'T FOR HUMANS, THE EARTH WOULD BE ALIVE AND WELL. AND YOU WANT TO SAVE IT?
Not my business, though.
NO, OUR AIM IS TO SAVE THE WORLD WITH THE POWERS OF TSUBASA.
SHE'LL DIE WHEN SHE CHOOSES. HUMANS AREN'T EVEN IN THE PICTURE.
NATURAL DISASTERS WEREN'T NEW ON THIS PLANET EVEN WHEN CIVILIZATION FLOURISHED.
YOU'RE...
YOU'RE AN INCREDIBLY SELFISH MAN...
THAT MEANS THAT THE EARTH LIVES AT HER OWN PACE.

...SO IT'S TRUE.
I DON'T WANT SOMEONE WHO ENGAGES IN SOME DODGY BUSINESS IN THE BASEMENT TELLING ME WHAT TO DO.
WHAT, DIDN'T YOU KNOW THAT?
Don't boast ...
DO I LOOK LIKE AN ANGEL?
AT LEAST...
I DIDN'T EVEN NOTICE THEM!!
YOU'RE NOT TO BE UNDER-ESTIMATED...
YOU DON'T KNOW HOW SURPRISED I WAS...
RAIMON SHIRAGI.
...TO SEE YOUR NAME IN THE ARMY'S DATABASE, WITH AN "E" ATTACHED TO IT.
?!
I WONDER WHAT BRINGS AN ELITE OFFICER DOWN HERE?

NO CAN DO. I WANT TO KEEP A LOW PROFILE, YOU KNOW.
I'M AFRAID YOU HAVE NO CHOICE. I KNOW YOU WERE IN CHARGE OF TOP-SECRET MILITARY OPERATIONS.
AND YOU NO LONGER WORK FOR THEM. WE SEE THAT AS A CHANCE.
!?
I can't believe I got an E!
!?
...YOU SEEM TO BE PRIVY TO A LOT OF INFO. YOU HAVE A COMPUTER IN THE BASEMENT OR SOMETHING?
MY GUESS IS THAT YOU HACKED INTO F, THE ARMY'S MOTHER COMPUTER.
THAT'S RIGHT. I'M HERE TO ASK YOU FOR HELP ABOUT IT.
GAH!
CRAP!
WE NEED YOUR HELP.
Wa--
--IT. HOLD IT, YOU...!

Raimon!!
I DID IT AGAIN.
DON'T BE SUCH A HERO!!
I'M DRAGGING HIM DOWN!!
RAIMON, DON'T LISTEN TO HIM!!
I'M SO STUPID!!
NOW, COME WITH US.
?!
...OKAY.
DO WHAT YOU WANT. I DON'T CARE!!
Butttface!!
NO WORRIES, KOTOBUKI.
RAIMON!!
WE WON'T, IF YOU DO YOUR JOB.
DON'T LAY A FINGER ON KOTOBUKI.

NOW...
I HAVE...
...JUST THE PLACE FOR YOU...
Place
WIND POWER GENERATOR
Sarabina Tower.
OW!
IT'S A LITTLE CRAMPED.
TRY TO MAKE YOURSELF AT HOME.
BASTARD...
KOTOBUKI?

Gya ha ha ha!
Ah ha ha ha!
SERVES HIM RIGHT!!
What a joke!
YOU'RE IN NO POSITION TO LAUGH!!
YOU GUYS ARE BEING HELD HERE, TOO?
SHOKA!!
And the others!
What's with those two...?
DUMA GOT HIM.
LOOK WHO'S TALKING! ANYWAY, WHERE'S RAIMON?!
Neighbors
LET ME TELL YOU ONE THING...
STAY PUT.
YOU CAN'T DO ANYTHING.
I...
RAIMON'S TOO GOOD FOR YOU.
JUST SIT PRETTY. THAT'S ALL YOU'RE GOOD FOR.

SHIT!
JUST CALM DOWN.
It won't open from inside.
WHAT DO YOU KNOW, YOU DAMNED TRANNIE!!
A TRANNIE...?
On what basis...?
No!!
I'M NOT GOING TO LET THEM TAKE HIM AWAY!!
I CAN'T LET THEM HAVE RAIMON.
NOT EVEN FOR A MINUTE!!
Wow.
Hey...
SKYLIGHT!!
Heyoo
WHY BOTHER? RAIMON WILL GET OUT OF THERE JUST FINE WITHOUT ANYONE'S HELP.
I'LL SHOW HIM. THEY CALLED ME MONKEY FOR A REASON!
I really don't care, though.

カリ
カリ
I DON'T WANT TO JUST BE TOGETHER.
...BE BETTER, AND...
YOU JUST WATCH!!
GAAAH...
WATCH OUT...!
"WHY ARE YOU UPSET?"
I DON'T WANT TO BE THE TAKER.
SO THAT I...
SO THAT...
...BECOME SOMEONE EVERYONE APPROVES OF.
I WANT TO HELP HIM. I WANT TO...

Grr
Well...
I HATE TO SAY THIS, BUT THAT'S NOT PRETTY...
YEAH ...
...I CAN PROTECT RAIMON!!
BOSS?
LET ME HELP YOU. WE CAN WORK SOMETHING OUT.
DON'T RUSH YOURSELF UNLESS YOU HAVE A PLAN.
HMPH.
YES!!
I JUST WANT TO MAKE DUMA PAY FOR PUTTING ME IN THIS PLACE.
IT'S NOTHING.
It's...
Huff
Huff
...WHY?
WAIT!!

I HEARD THAT DUMA HAS A COMPUTER IN THE BASEMENT OF THE SARABINA TOWER.
I THINK THAT'S WHERE THEY TOOK RAIMON.
I see.
THEY'VE GOT A COMPUTER. THUS THE NEED FOR ELECTRICITY.
'K...
どわわわ
DON'T DRAW WITH YOUR IRON NAIL!!
Skreee
Shoka!
THIS IS THE MAP OF THE TOWER.
BUT THERE'S EVEN BETTER WAY. IT'S THE POWER STATION.
AND WE'RE GOING TO SMASH THEM!!
...radiating as she spoke.
Her eyes were...
OKAY...
1F →
Door to the basement
...THE COMPUTER CONTROLS THE DOOR, SO WE COULDN'T OPEN IT.
THERE IS ONLY ONE DOOR LEADING DOWN TO THE BASEMENT. IT'S NOT THAT COMPLICATED. IT'LL BE A QUICK TRIP.
WE ALMOST MADE IT TO THE DOOR, BUT...
That's where they got caught.
B1 →
Raimon. Die, you idiot!

ALL RIGHT. ALL RIGHT!
KOTOBUKI, YOU'LL MAKE YOUR WAY TO THE DOOR AND WAIT. THREE MINUTES LATER, THE BOMBS WILL GO OFF, THE POWER WILL GO DOWN, AND YOU HEAD IN... ARE YOU LISTENING TO ME?!
WE'LL SET UP BOMBS IN THE GENERATORS.
THE SARABINA TOWER'S HERE, AND THE WIND GENERATORS, AND THIS IS HERE.
Sara-bina tower
Wind generators
You're here.
Boss...
I TOOK CARE OF THE GUARDS.
AND I GOT OUR WEAPONS BACK.
NOW, LET'S GO TO THE POWER STATION!
WHAT'S THAT?
IT'S SAFE TO ASSUME THEY HAVE A BACKUP INSTALLED.
By the way...
STAY ALERT EVEN WHEN THE LIGHTS ARE OUT.
I GOT IT. SO STOP SCRATCHING!!
How can you be so ignorant? How long have you been a thief? How can you so ignorant?
DON'T DILLY-DALLY. WHEN THE LIGHTS GO OUT, YOU GET IN THE DOOR. GOT IT?!
THEY'LL HAVE A TEMPORARY ELECTRICITY SUPPLY. WHICH MEAN THE DOOR WILL CLOSE SHORTLY AFTER.

HANG IN THERE, RAIMON.
Geez, why am I shaking...?
IT'S PAYBACK TIME, TRANNIE!!
It's her iron nails...
THANK YOU FOR YOUR PATIENCE...
RAIMON.
THANK YOU.
ANYTHING TO GET TO F.
IT GOT ME INFORMATION ON THE ARMY. I FOUND OUT A LOT ABOUT YOU, TOO, RAIMON.
.....
THAT'S SOME COMPUTER YOU'VE GOT HERE.

IT'S TOP-SECRET. IT'S DESIGNED TO BE.
HOWEVER, THERE'S ONE PROBLEM... THERE'S A POWERFUL BLOCK THAT'S PREVENTING ME FROM GOING FURTHER.
IT SEEMS IMPOSSIBLE TO BREAK. IT'S OBVIOUSLY IN A DIFFERENT LEAGUE.
TRUE! I THINK THIS MUST BE WHERE THEY HID TSUBASA!
OKAY... BUT YOU STILL HAVE TO DESTROY THE BLOCK.
I DON'T KNOW, AND I DON'T EVEN WANT TO KNOW.
WE'RE HOLDING KOTOBUKI HOSTAGE, REMEMBER?
TSUBASA IS NOT JUST A MYTH.
THE ARMY MUST BE ONTO SOMETHING.
IF YOU WANT TO SAVE THE WORLD, PLOW THE FIELDS AND PLANT SEEDS.
...THIS IS GETTING OLD.
WHY HIDE IT? TSUBASA IS OUR ONLY CHANCE AT SAVING THE EARTH.

SHE DOESN'T HAVE AN AGENDA LIKE ME.
IF KOTOBUKI THOUGHT LIKE YOU...
SHE NEVER STOPS TRYING.
...THAT WOULD BE WHAT SHE'D DO.
WE NEED A FOLK SONG OF HYOTAN ISLAND TO BEAK THE PASSWORD.
...OH, NO.
HUH?!
Hyotan? What's that?
...IF YOU DON'T WANT TO SEE HER DAMAGED, GET ON WITH IT.
I SAID DON'T TOUCH HER.
I'VE NEVER HEARD OF SUCH A--
Wh--
YOU DON'T KNOW? IT'S AN ISLAND OF AN ANCIENT COUNTRY CALLED JAPAN.
LIKE IT'S THE MOST NATURAL THING TO DO.

...CREATED THIS BLOCK.
STOP THAT.
OKAY, BUT YOU'D BETTER BE HAPPY WHEN WE GET IN.
GOTCHA.
NOT AT ALL. I WAS THE ONE WHO...
SAY THAT AGAIN WHEN YOU HAVE BROKEN INTO THE SYSTEM. IT MUST BE A HARD TASK EVEN FOR YOU...
THIS TIME IT'S TRUE.
RE-SEARCH ...?
WHEN YOU WERE 17...?
AS PART OF RESEARCH I DID WHEN I WAS 17.
RE--

IS EVERYTHING IN ORDER?
YES, SIR...
カシャン
!!
?!
WHAT'S THAT?!
DID YOU KILL THEM?
OF COURSE NOT. THEY'RE JUST GOING TO BE OUT FOR A WHILE.
GET THEM OUT.
I installed a fresh magazine.
Just light it before you shoot.
KOTOBUKI, YOU KNOW WHAT TO DO. YOU HAVE THREE MINUTES.
GET TO THE DOOR AND...GO INSIDE WHEN THE LIGHT GOES OUT.
SURE!
IF I FIND ANYTHING ABOUT TSUBASA, I WILL TAKE IT WITH ME.
YOU DO THAT, PLEASE. NOW GO!

IT'S HARD NOT TO LIKE SOMEONE LIKE THAT!!
WOW, I DIDN'T KNOW HELPING OTHERS WAS IN YOUR NATURE, BOSS.
Are you sure you're not sick?
SHE MAY BE DUMB, BUT SHE'S A GOOD GIRL...
...HEAD STRAIGHT.
Crud. There are guards...
I'VE GOT ONE MINUTE LEFT.
しゅたっ
I'M INSIDE THE TOWER...
"I'M JUST STEPPING ON YOU BECAUSE YOU'RE IN MY WAY."
MAKE A TURN THERE...
...AND...
Safe ...

WHAT?!
LET'S STEP ON THEM!!
ナムー
DID YOU... FAIL?!
IT'S PROGRAMMED THAT WAY. NO ACCESS FROM OUTSIDE IS ALLOWED.
WHA--
EVEN IF YOU GOT THE PASSWORD RIGHT...
...THE BLOCK WILL BE TURNED INTO A VIRUS.
IN 30 SECONDS, THE VIRUS WILL REACH YOUR COMPUTER...
...AND EAT IT UP.
IT WILL IDENTIFY THE LOCATION AND NOTIFY F IMMEDIATELY.

THIS IS WHY YOU DIDN'T PUT UP A FIGHT.
YOU HAD THIS PLANNED FROM THE BEGINNING...
DID YOU THINK YOU'D GET AWAY WITH IT?
NO REGRETS.
DIDN'T I TELL YOU?
!
AFTER YOU KISSED MY KOTOBUKI?
QUIT SCURRYING AROUND...
I CAN SEE THE DOOR...
RAIMON'S DOWN THERE...
YOU MUST BE DUMA'S ENEMY!

I HAVE TO GET TO THE DOOR SOON...!!
SEVEN SECONDS LEFT.
6
5
4
3
KA-CHAK
ガチッ
DO YOU WANT TO DIE?!
ビクッ
2
?!
ブッ
BEEP
.....
BACKUP SYSTEM IS ONLINE.

WHAT A TIMELY BLACKOUT... THE VIRUS IS DEAD.
IT LOOKS LIKE I AM IN LUCK.
FINE BY ME.
STOP RIGHT THERE.
YOU DON'T WASTE ANY TIME DO YOU?
カッ
I'VE GOT KOTOBUKI.
すっ

WHAT?
OH!
WHO'S THAT MAN LAYING THERE?
I SHOT HIM IN THE STOMACH ONCE, AND HE WENT FLYING INTO THE DOOR AND BROKE IT.
KOTOBUKI, YOU'RE HURT...
DON'T TOUCH ME!!
YOU'RE A REAL PIECE OF WORK.
...YOU HAD ME SO WORRIED WHILE YOU WERE GONE...
I KNEW YOU'D BE ABLE TO GET YOURSELF OUT...
...BUT...
YOU TOLD ME NOT TO WALK AWAY, AND LOOK WHAT YOU'VE DONE!!

YOU HURT HER, TOO, DIDN'T YOU?
OH...
NO!!
THE VIRUS IS ALIVE...
WHEN WE GET HOME, I'M GOING TO KISS EVERY PART OF YOUR BODY THAT HURTS.
RAIMON...
I'M SORRY I HURT YOU.
I'LL KILL YOU IF YOU TRY THAT...
RAIMON...
I'M DEAD.
THE VIRUS IS COMING...
?
OF COURSE.
YOU REALLY THOUGHT THAT MY VIRUS WOULD BE DESTROYED BY A MERE BLACKOUT?

HELLO!
I'M THE VIRUS'S CUTE LITTLE ANGEL, HERE TO PROTECT DATA FROM BAD PEOPLE!
HEY, YOU! YOU SHOULDN'T VIOLATE OTHER PEOPLE'S PRIVACY!
That is a big no-no.
I'M ALMOST AFRAID TO ASK... IS THAT ME?
Big no-no, my ass!
I MADE THIS WHEN I JUST MET YOU. YOU WERE SO ADORABLE, I JUST HAD TO USE YOU AS A MODEL.
It's cute, huh?
OH, AND THE ARMY IS GOING TO BE ONTO YOU.
THIS IS GOING TO BE A BIG TEARFUL REUNION.
IS THIS THE BEST YOU COULD DO?!
Kya ha ha!
I AM GOING TO PUNISH YOU, BAD BOY.
READY?!

WHA
SO LET'S DESTROY IT.
Uh...
YOU CAN STOP NOW! ONE MORE BLAST, AND THE TOWER WILL EXPLODE!
OH REALLY?
SOUNDS LIKE FUN TO ME.
IT'S NOT FUN AT ALL!!
THE TOWER IS GONE...
That's amazing...
IT'S RAIMON.
?!
DESTROYER!

NO NEED TO BE ANGRY. EVERYONE'S FINE.
And I only had to save Kotobuki.
DO YOU HAVE TO MAKE EVERYTHING SPECTACULAR?!!
Raimon!!
WH--
WHAT'S HAPPENING, RAIMON?!
DON'T ASK ME.
SHOKA.
YOU--!!
WHY DID YOU DESTROY THE TOWER?
WHAT IF THEY HAD A LEAD ON TSUBASA?!
BECAUSE DUMA HURT KOTOBUKI.
He deserved what he gets.
OH!
OW...
AH!
W-WHAT IS THIS?!
CRAZY NOISE FROM BELOW...

WHAT'S ...?
IT'S WARM...
IT'S A HOT SPRING...
HOT SPRING?
KYA!
HOT WATER FROM DEEP IN THE EARTH IS EXPLODING OUT OF THE GROUND!
Gasp
Came around
YOU MEAN...
THE EARTH IS STILL WARM...
HUH...?
I GUESS SO.
IT'S WARM. THAT'S PROOF OF LIFE, RIGHT?
UH-HUH.
HEY, TRANNIE. YOU HEAR THAT?

Raimon's shoes are very hard.

BESIDES, ALL THE EVIDENCE IS GONE ALONG WITH THE EXPLOSION.
I didn't mean it to happen.
Heh...
GEEZ...
HE'S SO SELFISH...
AND SO IS THE PLANET...
I am...
I'M SORRY...
I COULDN'T FIND A LEAD ON TSUBASA.

...LOOK GOOD TOGETHER.
...I THINK.
...YOU TWO KIND OF...
IT'S FINE. I HAD GIVEN UP HOPE FOR FINDING ANYTHING THE MOMENT THAT DEVIL SHOWED UP.
WELL, GOOD LUCK.
Let's go!
THERE'S BEEN ENOUGH DAMAGE FOR ONE DAY!!
Eek!
BOSS, RAIMON'S COMING!!
Well, anyway...
THIS GUY'LL GIVE US A LIFT TO THE NEXT VILLAGE.
Ye--
YES, SIR. MY PLEASURE!!
HUH?!
WHERE'S SHOKA?
SHE RA-- SHE'S GONE.
どぁ
Wait up, guys! Don't leave me behind!
Shake those legs, boss.
HE BLACK-MAILED HIM...
HM?
NOTHING...

Oh, that's...
!!
SHOULD I START WITH YOUR FACE?
YOUR HANDS? OR LEGS?
FIRST THING'S FIRST.
Now...
I'M GOING TO FIND WORK IN THE NEXT TOWN!
TELL ME EVERY SINGLE PART WHERE IT HURTS.
Oh?
WHAT FOR...?
STOP TRYING TO TRICK ME!!
Keep it down...
カッポ
WE MADE A PROMISE.
NOOO!!
WE'RE JUST GOING TO GO AND PLOW.
Eggs
Towel
WELCOME.
Cheap! Sarabina Springs
Massage service available
Duma, a few days later.

翼を持つ者
つばさ
も
もの

Adelite's Path

This is the girl who has received my undivided love, and she's going to make her first appearance in the third episode. To tell you the truth, I wanted to make her appear in the first episode, but when I finished plotting the story, my initial plan of her, her brother, and butler showing up had been eliminated. (laughter) And when I thought maybe this could be the chance to make them appear, I didn't have time to make it happen. It's sad, really.

There's another character I had to give up for a while after the second episode: Shoka. She was supposed to be a regular, but circumstances forced me to decide otherwise...

Here's Shoka in a maid costume.

Yeah!
BRING IT ON!!
THAT MEANS THEY'LL AT LEAST TALK TO ME.
WILSON HOUSE...
THEY PUT OUT AN AD LOOKING FOR A MAID.
EASY, KOTOBUKI. YOU'RE NOT GOING TO WAR OR ANYTHING.
THERE WERE SO MANY WARS...
...THAT CAUSED THE EARTH TO DRY UP.
Oh.
DON'T WORRY ABOUT THAT.
I'VE GOT TO ACT FAST BEFORE SOMEONE BEATS ME TO IT.
BUT I CAN'T HELP IT. OPPORTUNITY HAS FINALLY KNOCKED.
WE ARE IN THE 22ND CENTURY.
RAIMON...!
That's wrong...
I TORE THE AD OFF THE WALL.
You won't have any competition.
Wanted: Maid

ONLY THE RICH, THE ARMY, AND THE POLITICIANS HAVE ACCESS TO THE NICER AMENITIES.
MEANWHILE, ORDINARY PEOPLE LIVE IN POVERTY, AND THE STREETS ARE FILLED WITH CRIMINALS.
I'VE BEEN TRAVELING FROM TOWN TO TOWN, LOOKING FOR A JOB.
SOMEONE'S HERE FOR AN INTERVIEW.
knock knock
I LIVED AS A THIEF IN ORDER TO SURVIVE...
...BUT THAT'S ALL BEHIND ME, NOW.
THIS IS MY CHANCE!
WELCOME.
MY NAME IS ADELITE WILSON.
Oh?
What if it's someone like this?
But...

WHOA, YOU'RE...
I AM THE ONLY DAUGHTER OF THE FAMILY.
I AM GOING TO INTERVIEW YOU ON BEHALF OF MY LATE FATHER.
WOW.
Heh...
HONESTY WON'T WIN YOU ANYTHING, HONEY.
HUH?
RAIMON USED TO BE AN ELITE OFFICER IN THE ARMY.
HE'D CHASE AFTER ME IN HIS OWN FUSSY WAY WHEN I WAS A THIEF.
ONCE AGAIN... HUH?
She doesn't get it.
SHE'S RIGHT, KOTOBUKI. YOU KNOW WHAT THEY SAY... A CHILD PRODIGY'S A NOBODY AFTER AGE 20.
TWITCH
YEAH.
YOUR FRIEND?!
...WHO IS THAT?

Erm...
WELL, UM...
NO, IT'S NOT THAT.
I STILL CAN'T GET USED TO THAT IDEA.
YOUR BOYFRIEND?
SINCE THEN, WE'VE BEEN ON THE ROAD.
WHAT?!
HE QUIT FOUR AND A HALF MONTHS AGO, THOUGH.
HE SAID...
"ALL I WANTED WAS TO END THE WHOLE OFFICER-THIEF THING AND BE WITH YOU."
Four and a half months ago.
ANYWAY!!
Okay.
WE ARE SOUL MATES.
NOT ANOTHER WORD.
You're a bad liar.
I GET THAT A LOT! BUT LISTEN, I'M NOT THE TYPE!!
HAVING FUN?
AND I CAN UNLOCK ANYTHING. HIRE ME!!
In a matter of three seconds.
YOU'LL MAKE AN EXCELLENT THIEF.
I need a maid.
I'VE GOT THE SPEED...
ZP
...AND THE STRENGTH!
Hmph

THIS IS MY MOM.
...HELLO.
AND THAT'S DR. KAMIHARA. HE'S A SCIENTIST.
IS THIS YOUR NEW MAID?
OH, MY. THANKS.
Press the button, and it will speak.
That's life.
HERE'S A LITTLE SOMETHING FOR YOU.
MOTHER...
HE'S MAKING A DETECTOR...
How's that possible?
IT'S EASY TO JUST NAME IT THAT...
TSUBASA IS A MYTH.
WHEN IT'S DONE, WE'LL FIND TSUBASA AND WE WILL MAKE A LOT OF MONEY.
THAT'S ANOTHER CREATION FROM DR. KAMIHARA. ISN'T IT GREAT?
HE'S WORKING ON A TSUBASA DETECTOR RIGHT NOW, AND I'M SPONSORING HIM.
HUH? WHY? THERE'S NOTHING WRONG WITH BELIEVING IN TSUBASA.
THAT'S NOT THE POINT.
MOTHER!! DON'T START ON THAT AGAIN!!
That's life.

じ~
じ~
IT'S SAID THAT TSUBASA GRANTED EVERYONE'S WISHES.
NOBODY KNOWS WHAT IT LOOKS LIKE OR WHERE IT COMES FROM, BUT PEOPLE BELIEVE IT STILL LIES SOMEWHERE IN THE GROUND.
WHOEVER FINDS IT WILL HAVE HIS WISH GRANTED.
Eh?!
WHAT'S UP WITH HIM...?
OKAY THEN, MY LADY. I WILL EXCUSE MYSELF. I WILL KEEP YOU POSTED.
Please do!!
I'M JUST GOING TO SHOW HIM OUT.
Oh no!
I TRIPPED OVER SOMETHING.
ガチャン
びくっ
That's
GOD, THAT WOMAN REALLY TESTS ME.
OH, MY.
WATCH YOUR STEP...
ガシャン
That's life.

EH?
WE DON'T HAVE ANY OTHER CHOICE. YOU WERE THE ONLY APPLICANT.
IT SEEMS...
AND SHE'S WILLING TO SPONSOR THAT FRAUD.
HOW CAN SHE BELIEV IN A MYTH? TSUBASA !! JUST FICTIO
SO I'M GOING TO DECIDE: YOU'RE HIRED.
THAT WOMAN IS USELESS.
...THAT THEY DON'T GET ALONG.

Y!...
.....!!
WHO SAID ANYTHING ABOUT HIRING YOU?!
YIPPEE!!

AND SO...
OKAY, KOTOBUKI. YOU START WORK TOMORROW.
Yeah!
ASK ME ANYTHING!!
AS FOR RAIMON... ADY SAID YOU CAN DO WHATEVER...
HM.
It's a man.
Very nice.
ADY NEEDED TO GET HIRED HELP, WITH MOST OF THE ORIGINAL HOUSEKEEPERS GONE.
HER FATHER WAS AN EXECUTIVE AT A FABRIC MANUFACTURING COMPANY. EVER SINCE HE WAS KILLED IN A CAR ACCIDENT SIX MONTHS AGO...
You know.
...THINGS HAVE BEEN TOUGH FOR THE WILSONS.
We're feeling the pinch, too.
AS YOU'RE AWARE, THE LADY OF THE HOUSE IS NOT DEPENDABLE. SHE DOESN'T KNOW A THING ABOUT KEEPING FAMILY TOGETHER.
HOW CAN SHE BELIEVE IN TSUBASA AND THAT DODGY SCIENTIST? THAT'S JUST INSANE, DON'T YOU THINK?
You saw her, right?!
BUT ADELITE SEEMS SMART.
SHE'S A KNOW-IT-ALL. SHE DOESN'T TALK LIKE AN 11-YEAR-OLD CHILD.
SHE'LL NEVER GET MY SYMPATHY.
OH...
"ON BEHALF OF MY LATE FATHER..."

GRAB
!!
He's come back from a room allocated for him.
Kya!
YOU'LL FIND OUT WHAT I'M TALKING ABOUT TOMORROW.
.....
WHAT WAS THAT?!
WELL, YOU LOOKED LIKE YOU NEEDED CHEERING UP.
Out of the blue.
Hmph.
WHAT ARE YOU TALKING ABOUT...?
A job with a room and three meals! How can you ask for more?!!
I JUST GOT A JOB. IT'S A DREAM COME TRUE FOR ME.
But I insist!!
ANYWAY, WHAT MADE YOU COME HERE?
TO BE WITH YOU.
What else?
I'VE BEEN TELLING YOU, YOU DON'T HAVE TO DO THAT...
I'M GOING TO WORK MY BUTT OFF AND CLEAR UP MY DEBT!!
Raimon's been paying for the food and she wants to pay it back.

すくっ
Sorry I asked...
GOOD FOR YOU.
YOU'VE GOT A JOB.
HAPPY?
……
すく
I'm going to bed!!
WE HAVE A BIG DAY TOMORROW!!
ポン ポン
YEAH, LET'S.
SOMETIMES I THINK...
RAIMON SPOILS ME TOO MUCH!!
I JUST WANT TO BECOME GOOD ENOUGH FOR HIM. SOMEONE HE CAN COUNT ON!
I THINK!!
LIKE WHEN HE WOULDN'T LET ME...
BUT IT'S ALWAYS RAIMON WHO'S DOING THE PROTECTING.
I WAS HOPING I COULD GET HER IN THE MOOD...

HOLD ON!!
HE MIGHT FIND IT EASIER TO ACCEPT IF IT ISN'T MONEY!!
Right on, Kotobuki!!
YES! I COULD GIVE HIM A PRESENT!!
...AND MAKE HIM HAPPY...
...SPEND MY OWN MONEY FOR HIM.
I'll get you a new outfit.
I'll buy it myself!!
In other words, he tricked her into buying it.
BUT...
I WANT TO DO SOMETHING NICE FOR HIM.
WHEN I'VE EARNED ENOUGH MONEY...
...I WANT TO SPEND IT ON HIM...
All right!
LET'S START WITH ASKING HIM WHAT HE WANTS. AND DO IT SUBTLY.
LET'S WORK HARD!!
shoes on the bed!

"YOU MEAN, THERE'S A VENDOR TRYING TO CHEAT YOU?"
"I'VE BEEN GETTING SOME LOW QUALITY SILK, LATELY."
"REALLY?! THAT'S WONDERFUL!!"
"OUR COMPANY'S THROWING A PARTY NEXT MONTH. YOU SHOULD COME. WE'LL GET YOU A NEW DRESS."
"RIGHT. YOU HAVE CLUMSY HANDS."
"YOUR MOM CAN MAKE YOU ONE."
"OH, NO. I'M TERRIBLE WITH A NEEDLE AND THREAD. NO MATTER HOW HARD I TRY, I CAN'T GET IT DONE."
"MY LADY!!"
"ADY!! THERE WAS AN ACCIDENT AND MASTER WAS...!!"
"...I'M WORRIED."

"IT'S FOR DR. KAMIHARA. ONCE WE HAVE THE TSUBASA DETECTOR UP AND RUNNING, WE WON'T HAVE TO WORRY ABOUT MONEY."
"MOTHER!! WHAT IS THIS MONEY FOR?!"
"THE CLIFF CRUMBLED DOWN..."
"I WONDER IF THE LADY OF THE HOUSE WILL BE ABLE TO KEEP THE FAMILY TOGETHER..."
"MOTHER, YOU SHOULD STOP SPONSORING HIM. WE'LL BE BROKE IF YOU DON'T."
"I'M SORRY, MY LADY, BUT WE QUIT."
Wanted: Maid
"IT'S ALL RIGHT."
"IT'S ALL RIGHT."
BANG!

NO.
DON'T LOOK AT ME.
I KNOW I LOOK WEIRD!!
HOW CUTE!
OKAY, LET'S GET TO WORK.
RAIMON, YOU'RE IN THE BACK...
OH!!
YOU'RE SO LOVELY. I'M AROUSED.
You're kidding, right?
IT'S JUST A COSTUME!!
Huh?!

I WANT YOU.
In many ways.
FORGET IT!!
ハキッ
UM... IS THERE ANYTHING...
...YOU WANT...?
UM. I DON'T KNOW HOW TO START...
RAIMON, YOU'RE...
HM?
IT HAS TO BE A THING. A PHYSICAL THING.
YOU KNOW, SOMETHING YOU WANT TO OWN.
YOU.
ASIDE FROM ME.

SWITCH TO PLAN B. I'LL FIGURE IT OUT ON MY OWN.
WHAT WOULD IT BE...?
フキ
フキ
フキ
HE'S A TOUGH NUT TO CRACK.
I should have seen that coming.
とんっ
THAT'S NOT WHAT I ASKED!!
.....
Heh.

Anyway...
THIS IS SO MUCH FUN.
It's like a real job.
MOTHE--
KNOCK
MOTHER?
KNOCK
KNOCK
KNOCK
MOTHER?
NO!!
DON'T COME IN. GO AWAY!!
CLOSE THE DOOR!!
A LETTER FROM FATHER'S COMPANY.
OOPS.
OH.
ERM.
WELL...
Ah!
GIVE ME THAT!
THEN YOU SHOULD JUST ANSWER ME OR KEEP THE DOOR LOCKED.
YOU'RE RIGHT.
WHAT IS IT, DEAR?

IT'S AN INVITATION TO MR. PRESIDENT'S 60TH BIRTHDAY PARTY.
Really?
HOW NICE.
DON'T YOU GET IT? WE CAN'T AFFORD SOMETHING LIKE THIS ANYMORE.
YOU CAN SEND A MESSAGE CARD.
WHAT SHOULD I WRITE?

CONGRATULATIONS ON YOUR 60TH BIRTHDAY.
I PRAY THAT YOU WILL HAVE MANY MORE BIRTHDAYS TO COME.
WE ARE SORRY TO INFORM YOU THAT WE CANNOT PAY OUR COMPLIMENTS...

I KNOW WE HAVE SOMETHING GOOD HERE.
AND...

HUH?
...I'LL DO IT.

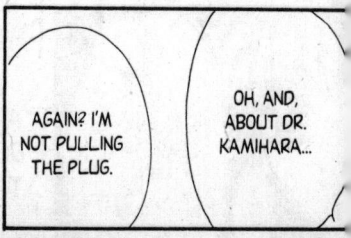
OH, AND, ABOUT DR. KAMIHARA...
AGAIN? I'M NOT PULLING THE PLUG.

IS THERE ANY OTHER WAY?
WELL...
.....!!
.....
Then...
I'LL WAIT FOR YOUR REPLY.
パタン
Kyaaah!!
WHAT?!
WHAT ARE YOU DOING UP THERE?!!
Kyaaah!
すたっ
WATCH OUT!!
Oh
SORRY.
Geez...
YOU MAY LEAVE THAT AREA...
.....

I HAVE NEVER BEEN AND WILL NEVER BE...
...A CHILD.
NOT THAT I CARE. I JUST HOPE...
...SHE STAYS OUT OF TROUBLE.
THAT'S ALL I ASK.
ADY... DO YOU HATE YOUR MOM
YOU WERE WATCH-ING US.
SHE HATES ME.
YOU SAW IT. SHE WOULDN'T LET ME IN.
SO WHAT ABOUT THE PARTY?
IT'S JUST NOISE. I HATE PARTIES.
Now...
IT'S FOODTIME!
.....
KOTOBUKI, AREN'T YOU HUNGRY?
BUT SHE LOOKED...
...A LITTLE...
SHE'S DEFINITELY SMART FOR AN 11-YEAR-OLD KID.

Omelet
IT'S TO DIE FOR!!
WOW!!
THERE'RE SO MANY THINGS I HAVE TO DO.
The omelet a big bonus.
Oh
MR. SHIRAGI.
GOOD.
GREAT.
HOW WAS YOUR FIRST DAY?
Hi.
SIT, SIT!
Really?
YOUR...
...BANDANA DOESN'T MATCH YOUR OUTFIT.
Can it really be called a bandana, though?
No idea.
THIS FEELS RIGHT FOR ME.
I GOT IT!!
Kyaaah!
THAT'S RIGHT.
DON'T TELL ME YOU'LL TURN VIOLENT WHEN YOU TAKE IT OFF.
Kyaaah!
HEH HEH...

Oh!
SORRY ABOUT THAT.
I DON'T KNOW WHAT CAME OVER YOU. YOU ALMOST KNOCKED THE TABLE OVER!
IT'S FINE AS LONG AS THERE'S FOOD FOR ME AND KOTOBUKI.

THAT'S IT. A BANDANA!!
KOTOBUKI.
IT'S NOT MUCH BUT IT'S A START!!

YOU ALL RIGHT?
YEAH. I'M FINE.

IT'S MORE FUN TO WORK...
...WHEN YOU HAVE A CLEAR GOAL.
OH?

...SILLY GIRL.

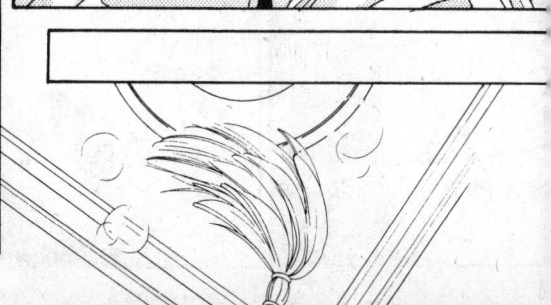

...I WONDER IF...
...LADY KNOWS SHE LOOKS...
...SO LONELY.
...HER MOM'S ROOM.
!
IT'S ADY... WHAT'S SHE LOOKING AT?
THATS...
NOT THAT I WOULD TELL HER THAT...
BUT... SHOULD I...
OH!
Hold on.
NO, BUT I WANTED TO...UH...
...I DIDN'T ASK.
SORRY, I JUST RAN HERE...
Huff
Huff
Huff
It's hard...
Huff
Huff
TEA.
I BROUGHT YOU TEA...
Huff
Huff
ADY!!
ひっ

HEH
OH!
HM?
YOU ARE AN ODD GIRL. OKAY, I'LL HAVE THE TEA.
RAIMON AND ADY'S MOM.
WAIT!
Okay...
And my favorite is Assam!!
Do you ever know how to brew tea? You ruined the flavor.
...I DON'T WANT IT.
NOT MY CUP OF TEA.
...AND I SAW YOU WEARING AN OLD BANDANA.
SO I GOT YOU A NEW ONE.
WHAT?

"NOT MY CUP OF TEA."
...THAT WAS MY IDEA.
...WHAT'S THE MATTER?
I WAS GOING TO GIVE HIM A BANDANA.
WAIT A MINUTE!!
YOU'RE A COUPLE, RIGHT?
THEN HE'S HAPPY JUST TO HAVE YOU.
WHY DON'T YOU LEAVE IT THAT WAY?

"THAT'S OKAY. THE DRESS YOU BOUGHT FOR ME IS MUCH BETTER."
"YOUR MOM COULDN'T MAKE YOU A DRESS."
I DON'T CARE ABOUT PRESENTS.
I'VE NEVER HAD ONE.
NOT EVEN A DRESS.
"I'M SORRY..."
"...JUST FOR ME."
ISN'T IT WONDERFUL?
Ah ha ha...
"WHAT A LOVELY DRESS!"
"MOM MADE IT..."
!!

KYAAAH!!
ADY?!
ハァハァ
WHAT?
THE CRYSTAL OUR FAMILY HAS CHERISHED FOR GENERATIONS IS GONE...!!
CRYSTAL?
WE HAD IT FITTED IN THE CEILING.
WHY...? WHERE DID IT GO?
KAMIHARA...!!
?
PROOF CAN FOLLOW LATER.
I'M NOT GOING TO LET HIM GET AWAY WITH IT!!
WAIT... DO YOU HAVE PROOF?
HE'S SO GOING TO PAY!!
OF COURSE. IT'S HIM.
HE WAS ALWAYS EYEING IT.

ADY, WAIT! CALM DOWN, WILL YOU?!
I AM BEING CALM!!
LET ME HELP!!
I CAN'T LEAVE HER LIKE THIS.
I'M COMING WITH YOU!!
...BUT TH DOESN'T CONCERN YOU.
I KNOW THIS IS UNCALLED FOR.
JUST LET ME!!
FINE.
SUIT YOURSELF.
SO THIS...
...IS HIS HOUSE. IT LOOKS SUSPICIOUS.
THAT'S WHAT I'VE BEEN SAYING FROM DAY ONE.

IT'S BETTER THAN MESSING UP AND CAUSING HIM TROUBLE.
IF I DON'T HAVE TO DO ANYTHING TO MAKE HIM HAPPY...
...THEN WOULD IT BE BEST TO LEAVE IT THAT WAY?
...I DIDN'T TELL HIM.
AT LEAST YOU DIDN'T BRING THAT WEIRD MAN WITH YOU. GOOD THINKING.
Avoiding.
He doesn't do work.
I COULDN'T FACE HIM...
I WANTED ONE WHEN I WAS A THIEF, BUT I DIDN'T HAVE THAT KIND OF MONEY...
*The electric version
Okay.
LET'S GO.
Wow!
AN EXPAN-DABLE LADDER!!
MAYBE I'LL JUST LET HIM SPOIL ME.
BUT...
...COULD I REALLY JUST LET HIM DO THAT?

WHAT A WEIRD PLACE...
THE CRYSTAL.
WHERE IS IT?
WHAT'S THIS...?
KYAAAH!! INTRUDERS!!
?!
WELL, WELL, WELL...
WHAT'S GOING ON?!
WAIT, THAT'S A ROBOT!!
WH-WHAT?!

KAMIHARA...
WE KNOW THAT YOU TOOK THE CRYSTAL!!
YOU GOT ME.
I KNEW IT!
...YOU SHOULD TRY AND DENY IT FIRST...
THE CRYSTAL IS ABSOLUTELY NECESSARY TO MAKE MY DETECTOR WORK.
THE INDEX OF REFRACTION IS SiO_2. THE CRYSTAL HAS A SUPERIOR QUALITY.
THIS IS NATURAL. A RARITY NOWADAYS. WHAT DO YOU SAY? CAN I HOLD ONTO THIS FOR A WHILE?
HOW CAN YOU BE SO COOL ABOUT IT!
I'M ONLY TALKING ABOUT THE GREATEST INVENTION OF THE CENTURY.
I WANT IT BACK NOW!!
HOW INTER-ESTING.
TELL ME HOW IT WORKS.
HOW SAD...

Oh no!! Someone else broke in!
YOU WERE FOLLOW-ING US?!!
RAI--
Kyaah!
Kyaah!
Kyaah!
I SAW YOU GOING OUT.
HERE'S YOUR LUNCH.
YOUR GREATEST INVENTION, THAT IS.
Kyaah!
Kyaah!
Kyaah!
Kyaah!
Kyaah!
Kyaah!
My little Remi?!
MY LITTLE REMI!!
Agh!
SHUT UP.

Remi...
YOUR NAME SOUNDED FAMILIAR.
YOU USED TO INVENT ONE USELESS WEAPON AFTER ANOTHER. IT TICKED THE ARMY OFF EVERY TIME.
YOU WERE AN IMBECILE THEN, YOU'RE AN IMBECILE NOW.
HOW...DO YOU KNOW ALL THIS...? ABOUT THE ARMY AND STUFF...
BECAUSE I'M A GENIUS.
WHAT DO YOU MEAN?
LOOK, I DON'T CARE WHATEVER CRAP YOU PULL, JUST LEAVE KOTOBUKI OUT OF IT.
For that reason I have to make you pay.
Wha--!
HOW DID YOU BREAK MY SECRET PASSWORD...?
I'M A GENIUS.
Mwa ha ha...
THAT'S NONSENSE. YOU GOT ANY EVIDENCE? I'M JUST A SCIENTIST WHO'S TRYING TO MAKE A DIFFERENCE IN THE WORLD.
Heh...
I'M AFRAID NOBODY BUT ME CAN GET IT MOVIN--
WE'LL SEE ABOUT THAT WHEN WE LAUNCH YOUR MACHINE.

どかーん
KYAAAH!!
IT'S OKAY. NO ONE LIVES THERE.
IT'S--
IT'S JUST A WEAPON!!
……
……
ひゅるるる
Damn.
IT'S YOUR FAULT. YOU LET ME DECEIVE YOU!!
YOU LIED TO US!!
WHY WOULD I LISTEN TO THAT BITCH?!
SHE WAS AN EASY TARGET. YOU'D BE BETTER OFF WITHOUT HER.
SHE'S NOT FIT TO BE A MOTHER.
HE'S RIGHT. SHE'S NEVER BEEN A GOOD MOTHER.
HEY!!
I DON'T CARE ABOUT TSUBASA. I WAS IN IT FOR THE MONEY AND THE CHANCE TO USE MY TALENTS.
WHAT'S THE PROBLEM? I THOUGHT YOU HATED YOUR MOTHER.

I'VE BEEN WAITING...
...FOR THE DAY WHERE I CAN SMILE LIKE THAT.
BUT...I'M DONE WAITING.
SHE CAN'T EVEN MAKE A DRESS...
I NEVER WENT TO ANOTHER PARTY.
I'VE BEEN WAITING.
SHE DOESN'T KNOW HOW TO TREAT A CHILD. SHE CAN'T EVEN CHANGE A DIAPER.
SHE'S CLUELESS, CLUMSY, AND SHALLOW.
I DON'T EXPECT ANYTHING FROM HER...
ADY.
IN TRUTH...
YOU KEPT YOUR TINY SELF ALL BOTTLED UP, DIDN'T YOU!?
I'VE SEEN THE LOOK...
...THAT SAYS "LOOK AT ME."
OH, NO, YOU DON'T.

!!
AGH!
HUH…?!
TWO…
…KOTO-BUKIS…?!
Nn?
THAT WAS SCARY.
KOTO-BUKI…?
UGH…
たたた
た

YOU OUGHT TO PROTECT ME.
Hey... I'm over here.
IF YOU LOVE ME, THEN SHOW IT.
YOU'RE HAPPY AS LONG AS I'M HERE, RIGHT?
!
What?!
WHAT AM I DOING...?!
EH?
AM I RIGHT?
SHUT UP!!
NO!! THIS IS NOT RIGHT AT ALL!!
THAT'S NOT ME!! IT'S NOT!
ブル
ブル
ブル
ブル
ブル
SHE'S WRONG!!
WHAT THE HELL IS SHE SAYING? SHE'S SO FULL OF IT!
ブル
ブル
だんっ
"I WONDER WHAT IT'S LIKE TO BE SPOILED?"

Oh, no!
THAT'S MY NEW ROBOT IN PROGRESS!!
IT'S NOT ME!!
That hurt a bit...
BE CAREFUL WITH THAT FIST OF YOURS! WHAT IF YOU WERE WRONG?
WHA--?!
ビボン
I knew you were a pervert.
BUT WHY KOTOBUKI...?
I LIKE THE WAY SHE LOOKS.
What are you--?!
STOP THAT!!
RIGHT.
THIS IS AN INSULT.
THEY DON'T LOOK ANYTHING ALIKE.
Kamikura

YOU CAN'T JUST QUIETLY WALK AWAY AFTER HURTING KOTOBUKI.
DIDN'T YOU KNOW THAT?
NO, I DID NO--
TOO BAD.
Gyaaaaah!!
WELL, HE DESERVES IT...
IT'S ALL RIGHT TO MAKE A MISTAKE...
OH?
THE FIRST TIME IS TRICKY.
BUT IT WON'T STOP ME...
I'LL KEEP TRYING UNTIL I CAN MAKE HIM HAPPY.
AND WHEN I CAN GET THAT SMILE...
...I WILL BE THE HAPPIEST PERSON.

...HAS THE POWER TO MOVE ME.
RAIMON!
YOUR SMILE...
WAIT!!
IF YOU MAKE ANOTHER MOVE...
...YOU'LL HAVE TO SAY GOODBYE TO YOUR CRYSTAL!!
So stop--Please?!
AND THIS IS ME MAKING AN EXIT. GOODBYE.
It's a runner!
NO...!
Hey!!
THAT'S MY CRYSTAL YOU'RE TALKING ABOUT!!
DO WHAT YOU WANT.
It's not mine.
PUSH IT.
It's not my house.
WHAT?!
WITH THE PUSH OF THE BUTTON, YOUR HOUSE IS ALL BUT GONE!!
OH, ONE MORE THING! I SET A BOMB IN WILSONS' HOUSE.
DON'T YOU DARE!!
HE CAME PREPARED!!

SHE CAN TAKE CARE OF HERSELF.
Eh?!
CUT THAT OUT!
GIVE IT BACK TO HER!!
YOU CAN'T MAKE HER STOP.
THAT'S DANGEROUS! AREN'T YOU GOING TO STOP HER?!
You're a lady, so act like one!
You sound like...
YOU SEEM TO KNOW EVERYTHING ABOUT HER.
...IS GOOD ENOUGH FOR ME.
BESIDES, SEEING HER ENJOYING WHAT SHE'S DOING...

GIVE ME THAT!
NO WAY! IT BELONGS TO ADY, YOU GREEDY MONSTER.
YOU LITTLE...!
GEEZ...
KOTOBUK!...
WATCH OUT, KOTOBUKI!!
TAKE...

KOTOBUKI, ARE YOU HURT?!
YOU HAVE BEEN WARNED.
CLICK
AHHHH!!
...INITIATIVE.
YOU MEAN...
...THE BOMB I REMOVED THE OTHER DAY?
COME ON, KOTOBUKI. LET'S GO.
FORGET IT. YOU WON'T MAKE IT TO THE WILSON HOUSE.
Not in 30 seconds.

...!...
WHEN DID YOU NOTICE THE BOMB...?
HM?
IT ALWAYS ENDS WITH A BANG.
TOGETHER WE CAN MAKE IT WORK...
IT'S YOU AND ME.
I'LL START BY SAYING WHAT I ALWAYS WANTED TO TELL YOU.
ARE YOU TALKING TO ME?
Yes!!
IS IT THAT HARD TO TELL?!
THANK YOU FOR THAT.
AND FOR TODAY.
IF IT DOESN'T WORK, I'LL COME UP WITH SOMETHING ELSE.
LIKE MAKING TEA.

Sigh...
NO. I CAN'T...
MOTHER!!
YOU JUST WAIT, MOTHER!
I'm going right after it.
I KNOW YOU'VE GOT ONE SCREW LOOSE, BUT LISTEN. I--
YOU CAN'T STOP ME ANYMORE.
Now that's determination.
ADY...
IT'S ALL RIGHT.
WHAT'S WRONG?! STOP THAT!!
Kyaah!

MOTHER ...?
DO YOU HATE IT?
I'M GETTING BETTER...
I'VE SEEN A LOT WORSE.
I...
But now you've seen it.
AH! I TOLD YOU NOT TO COME IN.
...
OH?!
I MESSED UP THE STITCHES, SO I THOUGHT I'D GIVE IT TO RAIMON INSTEAD, BUT HE DIDN'T WANT IT.
WHY WOULD I?
HOW...
...CONFUSING!!
That's life.

DID YOU USE THE OLD CALCULATOR? FATHER'S IS BROKEN.
The sleeves are different lengths.
Oh! Ah!
IT'S STILL TOO BIG FOR YOU. YOU'LL GROW INTO IT, EVENTUALLY.
I KNOW YOU STAY UP NIGHT AND STUDY.
YOU ARE NOT LIKE ME. I FEEL ASHAMED OF MYSELF.
I didn't know...
YOU'RE SO SMART, ADDY.
BUT I CAN TAKE CARE OF FINANCIAL MATTERS.
YOU CAN COUNT ON YOUR MOTHER!!
OH?
OH?!
ADY?

...
SHE'S TRYING, JUST WAY OFF.
がくっ
NO.
I MUST HAVE LET YOU DOWN WITH THE DRESS...
THIS IS...
...WHAT I WANTED...
THIS IS THE ONE...
THIS IS WHAT I'VE ALWAYS WANTED.
YOUR SMILE...

KAMIHARA WAS ARRESTED.
What? He was a fraud? Oh, my.
ADY AND HER MOM SOLD THEIR BIG HOUSE.
...YOU LOST YOUR JOB.
And...
What a shame. You looked so cute.
.....
...HAS THE POWER TO MOVE ME.
PLUS THE SALARY! I'LL FIND ANOTHER JOB IN NO TIME!!
NONE FOR ME.
How come?
IT'S OKAY.
Promise you'll write me when settled.
Promise.
I GOT ME A FRIEND.

There. I said it!!
I'LL BUY YOU A MEAL!!
SO TELL ME WHAT YOU WANT TO EAT!!
RAIMON...?
HM?
I...
SO... UM... YOU KNOW...
I KNOW THIS ISN'T MUCH, BUT...
IT WILL GET US SOMETHING TO EAT...
KOTOBUKI.
FORGET IT.
I WANT TO EAT AN OMELET.
AN OMELET.

.....
OKAY...!!
THAT CAN BE ARRANGED!!
HURRY, HURRY!!
I DIDN'T KNOW YOU LIKED OMELETS.
IT'S MY FAVORITE, TOO.
Let's tuck in.
YEAH.
MOTHER, I CAN'T GET KOTOBUKI'S IMAGE OUT OF MY HEAD...
WHAT'S WRONG WITH ME?
Oh, my.
THAT'S LOVE, ADY. LOVE.
My girl is suddenly grown up.

Wait, mom.

Welcome to the World of Tsubasa!

By the way, I have a cheongsam like this, but I haven't worn it yet. I wonder why I bought it...

◀ Anyhoo, let's go.

翼を持つ者
つばさ
もの

The Extra (One)

← Not a very catchy title.

GOOD. ANY EXCUSE FOR SLACKING OFF!!

Sweet!!

Don't worry about it. Nobody would miss it.

WE HAVE NO "KISS AND TELL" FOR THIS EPISODE.

The author had only one page for this.

Tsubasa wo Matsu Mono Volume 2

LOOK, YOUR MAN IS SOUND ASLEEP.

ホー

HOW CAN YOU SAY SOMETHING LIKE THAT AND NOT FEEL GUILTY?!

I'M JUST BEING BRAVE AND TELLING THE TRUTH.

BUT IT DOESN'T MAKE IT RIGHT!!

In the land of dreams.

EARTH IN THE 22ND CENTURY...
I'M SURE. IT'S RAIMON SHIRAGI.
...RIGHT. I WASN'T EXPECTING...
SIR, WE HAVE A NOTE ON THE GIRL FROM "F".
RAIMON TRAVELING WITH SOMEONE IS INTERESTING ENOUGH.
THIS IS EVEN BETTER.
KLAK

THE THIEF KOTOBUKI...
LOOK.
IT'S THE SEA!
RAAAIMON!
YOU'VE NEVER SEEN IT BEFORE?
NOPE! CAN WE CAN GO IN?
I THINK IT'S STILL POLLUTED.
POLLUTED?!

FIELDS AREN'T THE ONLY THINGS THAT GOT HIT HARD DURING THE WARS.
HMM...
I'M HUNGRY.
WANNA GRAB SOMETHING IN TOWN?
UM...
BUT... YOU'RE GOING TO PAY AGAIN...
DON'T WORRY ABOUT IT.
JUST GIVE UP. YOU'LL NEVER BE RICH.
Not a chance.
Maybe you're right.
Happy now?
HOLD ON.
I HAVE AN IDEA.
YEAH?
?
LOOK. WE'VE BEEN ON THE ROAD FOR SOME TIME AND WE'RE STARVED. WE REALLY COULD USE YOUR HELP. A WALLET WILL DO--
THAT'S YOUR IDEA?!
THERE WERE SO MANY WARS...

BY THE START OF THE 22ND CENTURY, THE FIELDS WERE WITHERED AND THE EARTH WAS IN A STATE OF DESOLATION.
ONLY THE RICH, THE ARMY, AND THE POLITICIANS HAVE ACCESS TO THE NICER AMENITIES.
MEANWHILE, ORDINARY PEOPLE SUFFER IN POVERTY AND CRIME IS COMMON.
I'M SICKLY...
...AND WEAK.
AND I ONLY MAKE MYSELF USEFUL FOR KOTOBUKI.
I WAS A THIEF IN ORDER TO SURVIVE, BUT IT'S ALL BEHIND ME NOW.
I'M TRAVELING FROM TOWN TO TOWN, LOOKING FOR A JOB.
WOULD YOU HIRE ME?!
NO GIRLS, BUT WE MIGHT NEED A GUY. WHAT DO YOU SAY, BUDDY?
I COULD DO A 100 TIMES BETTER THAN HIM!!
How about that?!
SORRY, NOT INTERESTED.
RAIMON SHIRAGI USED TO BE AN ELITE MILITARY OFFICER.

WE'VE BEEN TRAVELING TOGETHER FOR FIVE MONTHS, NOW.
HE KIND OF CHASED AFTER ME WHEN I WAS A THIEF...
...BUT HE QUIT THE ARMY SO WE COULD BE TOGETHER.
I WANT TO BE GOOD ENOUGH FOR RAIMON, SOMEDAY.
THE ARMY IS THE PLACE ONLY FOR THE PRIVILEGED FEW...
...AND RAIMON WAS A YOUNG CAPTAIN WITH A PROMISING CAREER.
HE HAS A TATTOO ON HIS LEFT CHEST TO PROVE IT.
SO HE CAN COUNT ON ME.
IN ORDER TO DO SO, I HAVE TO FIND HONEST WORK.
I NEVER THOUGHT GETTING A JOB WAS SO DIFFICULT!!
Can jobs even play hard to get?!
BUT...

If we work together, robbing could be fun.
YOU CAN DEPEND ON ME.
.....
BUT YOU'RE PAYING AGAIN...
Want a fish cake?
RELAX AND ENJOY YOUR MEAL.
With ※clean money, fortunately.
She stopped him earlier
YOU DON'T NEED TO TRY SO HARD.
STOP FIGHTING IT.
Wh-
WHAT THE--!!
WHAT IS HE SAYING?
Stop that!
STOP MANIPULATING ME TO SUIT YOUR NEEDS!!
Grr!
I'm not joking.
Oh!
IS THAT ANY WAY TO TREAT YOUR LOVER?
PAT

WORD HAS IT THAT TSUBASA ONCE LANDED HERE.
REALLY...?
I couldn't resist.
WE SHOULD DO SOMETHING ABOUT YOUR WANDERING HAND.
FEEL FREE TO TOUCH ME ANYWHERE, IN RETURN. ♡ ♡
ぎゅ ぎゅ ぎゅ ぎゅ ぎゅ
THIS LAND USED TO BE FERTILE...
LET'S BLAME THE HARD TIMES!!
Blame the poverty.
んんん!!
IN YOUR DREAMS!!
OUCH, THAT HURT.
Now I'm sad.
TSUBASA IS A MYTH OF OUR TIME.
SOME PEOPLE BELIEVE THAT IT'S HIDDEN AND THAT WHOEVER FINDS IT WILL HAVE A WISH GRANTED.
IT'S SAID TO HAVE SHOWN UP ONE DAY, AND THEN VANISHED AFTER GRANTING EVERYONE'S WISHES.
Wow...
You think?
SOUNDS LIKE A MYSTERIOUS PLACE.

THIEF!!
ひくっ
WHO IS IT?!
I nearly had a heart attack!!
Ah ha ha!
EAT THIS!!
!!
IT WASN'T ME!
RELAX, KOTOBUKI.
Poor girl...
Kyaaah!
ドボ
.....
!!

LET'S GO.
YEAH.
A CHILD...!!
KOTOBUK!...
MY CHILD... MY CHILD...
KONG
OUCH!
Mama!
W-WAIT!!
HURRY!!
COME ON!!

ARE YOU HURT?
NO...
AIRA...
THEY LEFT...
...SOMETHING BEHIND...
!
THEY CAN'T BE ON THE ROOF...
STAY OUT OF IT.
I KNOW!
GEEZ...
THEY'RE ALREADY GONE.

Oh!
MY BAD.
I'M IN A HURRY.
Sorry!
……
ゴーン
ゴーン
ゴーン
WHA--
WHAT JUST HAPPENED?!
くらっ
ふらふら

I CAN'T THANK YOU ENOUGH...
I DIDN'T DO ANYTHING.
I didn't even try.
THANK THE LADY OVER THERE. THE ONE WHO KEEPS BRUSHING HER TEETH...
Sniff
Sniff
Sniff
THANK YOU SO MUCH.
IT'S A GROUP OF PEOPLE WHO HAVE A THING AGAINST THE MILITARY REGIME.
HM...
NOZING NOZING.
*Nothing nothing.
WHAT'S WRONG?
RESISTANCE?
THEY'RE A RESISTANCE FORCE CALLED THE TEKI. YOU CAN TELL BY THE BANNER. THEY HAVE A HIDEOUT NEAR THE BEACH.
IT'S OKAY. ANYWAY, WHAT'S UP WITH THEM?!

THEY STARTED TO RESORT TO VIOLENCE ABOUT A WEEK AGO...
...TO GET THE MESSAGE OUT
.....
THE WORLD HAS GONE THOUGH A BIG CHANGE SINCE THE 21ST CENTURY, BUT THIS MAP WOULD SUFFICE.
THIS IS OUR COUNTRY, KNEELS.
DUVENI AND SOME OTHER SMALL COUNTRIES ARE RUN BY MILITARY, TOO.
*I improvised.
I GUESS NO COUNTRY IS WITHOUT A RESISTANCE
IT MEANS "NOT POSSIBLE."
THE ARMY USUALLY CALLS THEM "BLUE ROSE."
.....

THIS IS ONE OF THOSE TIMES WHERE I'M REMINDED THAT HE WAS IN THE ARMY.
...ARE THEY GONNA STOP THEM?
DON'T WORRY ABOUT THE ARMY.
THEY'RE NO STRANGER TO FOUL PLAY.
I WASN'T PART OF HIS LIFE BACK THEN.
SO WE'RE GOING TO SIT AROUND AND DO NOTHING?
NOT FOR NOW. THEY'RE EASILY PROVOKED. THE GROUP'LL CRY MILITARY BRUTALITY UNLESS THE ARMY HAS SOMETHING SOLID ON THEM.
Duveni is another story.
.....?
I'VE NEVER SEEN A WORLD MAP BEFORE. IT'S AMAZING.
THE WORLD IS SO BIG.
NOT JUST YET.
Wait.
CAN I ERASE THE MAP?

THE WORLD IS SO BIG AND I'M JUST A TINY DROP IN THE BUCKET.
Hmm...
TEKI'S WREAKING HAVOC WITH THE TOWN...
DO YOU HAVE ANY PLANS FOR JOB HUNTING TOMORROW?
OH, SHOOT. I STILL HAVE THAT BANNER.
I'LL GET RID OF IT.
I'm using your lighter.
I'M JUST GOING TO GO AND SET IT ON FIRE.
I DIDN'T DO IT ON PURPOSE!!
IT WAS AN ACCIDENT. IT JUST HAPPENED!!
WHAT WERE YOU BRUSHING YOUR TEETH FOR?

HE'S GOING TO HATE ME WHEN HE FINDS OUT!!
No....
HEY!!
WHAT ARE YOU BURNING OUT HERE?
BUT...
...I STILL KISSED SOMEONE OTHER THAN RAIMON.
OH....
...MY GOD!

OFFICERS!!
WHAT HAVE WE GOT HERE?
Has a habit of running at the drop of a hat.
THIS...
YOU'RE...
He put out the fire with his foot.
ARE YOU A MEMBER OF TEKI?
WHAT?!
NO WAY!!
WAIT A MINUTE!!
YOU GOT IT ALL WRONG!! I FOUND IT ON THE STREET!!
RESISTING ARREST...
THAT LEAVES ME WITH NO CHOICE.
I HEARD YOU MADE QUITE A SCENE TODAY.
TAKE HER.
WAI--

Ka-chak
UCH--!
DON'T WORRY. IT'S NOT POISON.
IT'LL JUST MAKE YOU A BIT SLEEPY AND URGES YOU TO TALK.
HEY!!
HANDS OFF.

だん
Hey...!
WHAT ARE YOU--?! GET OFF!!
ぐい
くる
RAI...
I COULD...
...SHAKE HIM...
...EASILY...
...OFF.

WHAT'S THIS?
ガク
ガク
ガク
ガク
ガク
ガク
WH--
YOU'RE SAFE NOW...
pat
Now.
WHO SHOT HER?
No drug works on Raimon.
I DID!!
NOW DON'T MAKE THIS ANY HARDER!!
SHE'S MINE.
STAY CLEAR, GOT IT?

CAPTAIN...
WHAT'S WRONG WITH ME...?
I DON'T HEAR A "YES, SIR."
SHI--
CAPTAIN SHIRAGI...?!

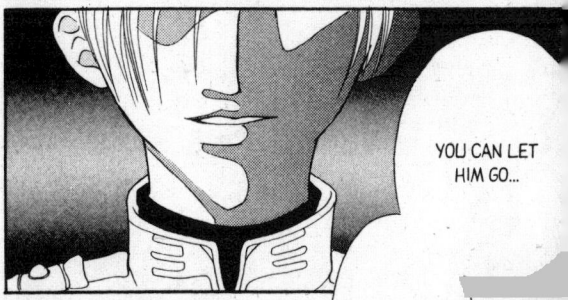
YOU CAN LET HIM GO...

...RAIMON.

Sigh...
HERE COMES MAJOR TOYA INGRAM.
MA... JOR?
A POSITION MUCH ABOVE CAPTAIN.
WHAT?!
WHAT BRINGS HIM DOWN HERE...?
LONG TIME NO SEE.
RAIMON...
LOOK WHO'S TALKING.
THIS IS A NEW LOW...
...EVEN FOR YOU, TOYA.
Yikes!
First name basis?!

ピ
NO.2416: DATA ON KOTOBUKI CLEARED.
Listen!
I'M NOT A MEMBER! ALTHOUGH THE THIEF PART IS TRUE...
FROM WHAT I HEAR, SHE'S A MEMBER OF TEKI.
THE GIRL YOU TOOK UNDER YOUR WING IS LISTED AS A THIEF IN F'S DATABASE.
*F is the Army's mother computer
OH?! CAPTAIN SHIRAGI?!
LET GO.
HOW STUPID.
Oh.
I ALMOST FORGOT.
……
Sigh...
GEEZ... YOU MANIPULATE F SO EASILY, RAIMON.
HOW COULD YOU DO THAT, CAPTAIN SHIRAGI?!!
ムムムム!
I FORGOT TO ERASE IT.

IF YOU'RE TRYING TO GET ME THROUGH KOTOBUKI, YOU'D BETTER THINK AGAIN.
YOU HAVEN'T CHAN--
Hah hah...
IT'S PART OF MY JOB.
WE'VE BEEN KEEPING AN EYE ON TEKI. THEY'VE BEEN ACTING UP A LOT, LATELY.
.....
.....
...I GUESS YOU STILL HATE IT WHEN SOMEONE TOUCHES YOUR HAIR.
GO UNDERCOVER INTO TEKI AS A MOLE.
HOW DOES THAT SOUND?
HUH?
YOUR GIRL IS STILL A SUSPECT AS A MEMBER OF TEKI.
I SAID I AM NOT!!
Did you hear me?!
CONVINCE ME, YOUNG LADY. GIVE US SOMETHING TO WORK WITH.
SAY...
ARE YOU DEAF?!

mumble
YOU KISSED ANOTHER GUY, DIDN'T YOU?
TOYA!
SORRY, RAIMON. COMES WITH THE TERRITORY.
SO?
BUT I DON'T WANT TO BE A SPY...
Oh...
THAT'S RIGHT...
SORRY, RAIMON.
GIVE ME MORE DETAILS!!
Over there!
H-h-how...
HOW DID YOU KNOW THAT?!
I WAS PASSING.
STUPID. IT'S JUST MY WORD AGAINST YOU.

RAIMON WAS...
...LIKE A FLOWER TO THE COLONEL AND ME.
OH?
HE WAS OUR JOY. SEEING HIM GROW EACH DAY.
Heh...
HE ALWAYS HAD A CHIP ON THE SHOULDER. I ADORED HIM.
WHY DIDN'T I THINK OF THAT...?
BUT YOU CAME ALONG AND BROKE THE FLOWER.
No photos for you.
NOW YOU'VE LOST ME...
Oh, well.
HE'S A BIT OFF...
THESE ARE HIS PHOTOS FROM HIS CHILDHOOD. OH! HE HAD SUCH LOVABLE GLARE.
IF I HADN'T DEPORTED HIM...
...HE WOULD HAVE MADE A FINE LIEUTENANT BY NOW.

LET ME BE STRAIGHT WITH YOU. I DON'T LIKE YOU.
ZSSH
HOW SAD. AND YOU CLAIM TO BE HIS LOVER?
RAIMON'S?
LIEUTENANT...? I THOUGHT HE WAS ON THE POLICE FORCE FROM THE GET-GO.
I TAKE IT YOU DON'T KNOW MUCH ABOUT RAIMON AS AN OFFICER.
I WILL GET RAIMON BACK.
NOW, TEKI HAS STARTED ROBBING ALL OVER THE TOWN.
I'D LIKE FOR YOU TO HELP US NAIL THEM. GET US SOMETHING GOOD.
NOOO!
AND...
IF YOU FAIL, I'LL TELL HIM ABOUT THE KISS...
...and have you arrested.

BASTARD!!
BRING IT ON.
YOU JUST WATCH.
...WELL?
B--
All 20 volumes.
GET LOST.
IF YOU SUCCEED, I'LL LET YOU KNOW EVERYTHING THERE IS TO KNOW ABOUT RAIMON.
STARTING WITH MY PRIVATE DIARIES.
Heh heh...
GOOD LUCK.
GOOD. TEKI'S BASE IS BEHIND A CRAG NEAR THE BEACH.
THIS IS THE MAP. YOU WILL HAVE TO FIND YOUR OWN WAY IN, WITHOUT ANY HELP FROM RAIMON.
YOU DON'T HAVE TO TELL ME!

THAT'S NOT MY PRIORITY!!
I'M NOT GOING TO...
...HAND HIM OVER!!
TOYA WAS DEAD SERIOUS.
HE WANTS RAIMON BACK SO BADLY...
MY INNOCENCE?
HAND OVER WHO?
SO WHAT DID TOYA WANT? ARE YOU REALLY GOING UNDERCOVER?
Um?
YEAH... I GUESS.
Clear my name once and for all.
NOTHING.
Meow!
FOR YOUR INNOCENCE
FOR RAIMON.
SO THE ARMY...
...HAS UNFINISHED BUSINESS WITH RAIMON...

I AM NOT GOING ANYWHERE.
OKAY...
STAY OUT OF THIS. THIS IS MY PROBLEM, NOT YOURS...
IT'S ALL RIGHT.
I GET IT. I'LL STAY ON THE SIDELINES.
JUST RE-MEMBER...
YOU DON'T HAVE TO HIDE ANYTHING FROM ME.
I WON'T LET THEM TAKE HIM AWAY.
I KNOW...
I WON'T...

UNDERSTAND?
YOUR NECK IS SO THIN...
SUCH BIG...
...HANDS.

UGGGH!
Ouch...
WHY?!
I'M GOING FOR A WALK!!
...START SHAKING?!
WHY, WHY, WHY?!
IT'S NATURAL.
HOW COULD I BE SO NAÏVE?
WHY DID I...

ARE YOU SURE ABOUT KOTOBUKI...?
WELL, OUR ASSIGNMENT IS TO BUST TEKI AND FIND THAT THING.
ARE YOU READY FOR THIS?
RAIMON IS A MAN.
BUT...JUST THINKING ABOUT HIM MAKES MY KNEES GO WEAK.
YAN MIZUCHI...
THE HEAD OF TEKI.
MAJOR INGRAM...

HUH?!
YAN, SOME OF THE FANS THINK YOU HAVE THE HOTS FOR KOTOBUKI.
How come?!
ハッキ
SHOKA!!
IT'S NOT TRUE! THEY'RE WRONG! CALM DOWN!!
Don't run away!!
ゆらめ
……

翼を持つ者
つばさ　もの

WE'D FOOL AROUND, BUT IT NEVER MADE ME SELF-CONSCIOUS.
E CAN DO ANYTHING, AND HE'S SMART.
I THOUGHT OUR DIFFERENCES STOPPED THERE.
IT WASN'T LIKE THIS BEFORE.
MAJOR...
WE HAVE RECEIVED SOME FOX FROM THE HEADQUARTERS.
GOOD.
LET'S GET THIS SHOW ON THE ROAD.

BUT NOW THAT I'VE REALLY LOOKED... HE'S A MAN.
KOH, THE FORMER HEAD OF TEKI, DIED TWO MONTHS AGO.
HIS SON, YAN MIZUCHI, TOOK OVER. THE GANG HAS 50 MEMBERS.
THAT'S ABOUT IT.
Huh?!
OH, RIGHT!!
CRAP! I'VE GOT TO FOCUS ON BUSINESS AT HAND!!
Wow...
THIS IS A DANGEROUS PLACE TO BUILD A HIDEOUT.
SO ARE YOU GOING TO SNEAK IN?
I'M STILL THINKING... YOU SAID YOU'D STAY OUT OF THIS, REMEMBER?
はあぁ

YES! DON'T PLAY DUMB!!
I DID?
TO CLEAR MY NAME AS AN ACCOMPLICE OF TEKI...
...AND, MORE IMPORTANTLY...
"IF YOU FAIL, I WILL TAKE RAIMON BACK."
THAT WAS THE PROMISE I MADE WITH TOYA.
I AM TO INVESTIGATE WITHOUT ANY HELP FROM RAIMON.
...TO KEEP HIM AWAY FROM RAIMON!!
Grrr!
IF I CAN'T...
KOTOBUKI, LISTEN.
I PROMISE I WON'T DO ANYTHING. SO CAN I STAY, PLEASE?
...I'LL GO OUT OF MY MIND.

EARTH TO KOTOBUKI.
THE STRENGTH...
THAT DEEP VOICE...
THAT BODY...
THOSE HANDS...
HE'S SO DIFFERENT FROM ME!!
WHY ARE YOU ALL BUNDLED UP?
Aren't you hot?
OH, THIS? I-IT'S NOTING
odd pose
I CAN'T TELL HIM I FEEL SHY.

Kyuuun!
THE SHAKING HAS STARTED AGAIN!!
HOW COULD I NOT FEEL ANYTHING BEFORE?
WAIT.
SOMEONE'S COMING.
OH.
IT SEEMS IMPOSSIBLE THAT HE'S EVEN KISSED ME ALREADY.
IF HE KISSES ME NOW...
WHAT?!
I WAS HOPING WE COULD GET THEM TO TALK AND GET IT OUT OF THE WAY QUICKLY.
...I'LL EXPLODE!!
THEY'RE NOT HERE. THOSE TWO GUYS WE SAW IN TOWN YESTERDAY.
They're gone.
I CAN SEE ONLY A FEW OF THEM.
MAYBE THEY'RE OUT ROBBING...
MAYBE.

There're things to do before going in.
.....
...I'LL GO BACK TO TOWN...
YEAH...
.....
ANYWAY...
HOW AM I GOING TO PROTECT RAIMON LIKE THIS...?
GOTCHA.
I'LL JUST GO AND LOOK AFTER SOMETHING...
Wants it.
Phew...

I'M JUST CURIOUS...
Eh heh...
EFINITELY NOT ME...
Clothes
WHAT A CUTE DRESS...
I'VE NEVER WORN A DRESS LIKE THAT...
I'VE NEVER SEEN YOU WEARING THAT KIND OF DRESS.
WHAT?!
Ahh... Um...
OU'LL LOOK GREAT IN IT. YOU'RE ALREADY PRETTY.
YOU LOOK LOVELY.
I'M GOING CRAZY...
N-
NO.

...AND IT'S GETTING WORSE!!
HELLO...
...TO BOTH OF YOU.
Yikes!
TOYA!!
Aren't you two hot?
JUST A MEAL....?
EASY, BOY.
WANNA HAVE A MEAL WITH ME?
Heh...
OF COURSE.
YOUR FACE SAYS...
..."FOR NOW," YOU JERK.

Oops.
MY BAD...
!!
WHAT'S WITH HIM...?
WHAT AN ODD SCENT...
AH!
...FROM YESTERDAY!
Yesterday
Ah ha ha!
IT WAS A CLOSE CALL, WASN'T IT? WE ALMOST KISSED.
OH...
YOU AGAIN.
IT'S YOU...

YAN!
HEY. HOW'S IT GOING?
TOO EARLY TO TELL...
BUT I KNOW WE'LL OUTSMART THEM...
I CAN BET YOU THAT.
DON'T THEY HAVE MORE IMPORTANT THINGS TO DO THAN GOING AFTER US?
SLACKERS.
DON'T WORRY ABOUT IT. WE SHARE THE SAME PAIN.
HEY...
NEXT TIME, LOOK WHERE YOU'RE GOING.
Bye!!
WAI-
Hold on a sec!
YOUR... GIVE ME YOUR NAME!!

OH DEAR. DON'T MAKE ME ARREST YOU...
Sigh...
I FEEL SORRY FOR THOSE GUYS IN TEKI.
The Army is full of jerks.
SO...
HOW'S YOUR INVESTIGATION GOING, KOTOBUKI?
YOU DON'T KNOW WHAT YOU'RE SAYING.
Heh heh...
I JUST STARTED. NOT MUCH I CAN DO IN ONE DAY.
THAT'S THE RESULT OF HUMAN BEINGS TIPPING THE BALANCE AND TRYING TO RUN THE PLANET.
LIFELESS OCEAN THAT LIGHT DOES NOT PENETRATE.
IT BEARS A SIMILARITY TO WHAT BLUE ROSE STANDS FOR.
HAVE YOU SEEN THE SEA HERE?

THIS COUNTRY WOULD FALL APART WITHOUT THE ARMY.
TO LOOK FOR CHANGE MEANS...
WHAT ELSE CAN KEEP IT TOGETHER?
...DESTROYING THE PEACE.
IT WOULDN'T LAST A YEAR.
CHANGE...
BY THE WAY...
HOW FAR HAVE YOU TWO GONE?
"CHANGE"...

IT DIDN'T MATTER...
IT DIDN'T MATTER...
...BE...
...FORE.
What?!
なっ
...old goat.
Don't point your finger at me, son.
NAUGHTY ...
I WAS JUST CURIOUS.
Really.
WHAT IS IT TO YOU?
I-IT'S--
KOTOBUKI.
I'VE CHANGED.
MY FEELINGS FOR RAIMON ARE CHANGING...
ガタン
LEAVE ME ALONE!!
.....

KOTOBUKI.
...IN A VERY STRANGE WAY!!
NO...!
OH...
I--
I'M SORRY...
I'M SO... SORRY...

I HURT HIM...!!
SORRY...
I COULD DIE.
I DON'T GET IT, RAIMON...
WHAT DO YOU SEE IN HER?
SHE'S JUST A CHILD. SHE CAN'T HELP BUT PLAY GAMES.
...YES.
HM?

SHE'S SO CUTE I COULD JUST DIE...
"No!"
SHE HASN'T HAD A CHANCE TO LEARN THE THINGS YOU DO WHILE GROWING UP.
SHE GREW UP ALONE.
Not pleased.
SHE'S SO INEXPERIENCED.
.....
I'M GOING TO TURN HER INTO A WOMAN.
THAT'S WHY SHE'S SO NAÏVE.
BUT...
THE EMPTINESS I USED TO SEE IN THEM IS GONE.
THERE'S A CALMNESS IN YOUR EYES...
.....

GO AHEAD AND TELL HER.
BYE.
RAIMON...
I MISS THOSE EYES...
I WONDER HOW SHE'D FEEL IF SHE KNEW ABOUT THE OLD YOU.
sniff
sniff
sniff
THIS IS WHERE OUR DREAM LIVES...
.....

IS THIS...
"TO LOOK FOR CHANGE MEANS DESTROYING THE PEACE."
...THE END OF OUR RELATIONSHIP?
NO... PLEASE, NO...
I HURT HIS FEELINGS. WHAT DID I HIT HIM FOR?
I'M GOING THROUGH A CHANGE.
WHY...?
HAVE I CHANGED BECAUSE I WANTED ALL OF THIS TO END?
MAYBE IT IS. I CAN'T ACT CASUAL AROUND HIM ANYMORE.
WHAT WAS...?
WHAT DOES TEKI WANT TO CHANGE BY DESTROYING...
...WHAT WE HAVE?
ぴっ
どお

ぴた
……
NOW THEY'VE DONE IT...
No finesse...
ゴオオ
Kyaaah!
ワアアア
IT'S TEKI...!
THEY'VE DONE IT AGAIN!!
ワア
IT'S ON FIRE...
WHY...
...DESTROY WHAT WE HAVE?
I HAVE TO...
...PUT OUT THE FIRE...
た

Oh--
OH MY GOD...
BACK OFF.
A BOMB?!
Ah!
IT'S YOU...!
YO.
WHY ARE YOU HERE...?
YAN!
THE UPPER SIDE OF IT LOOKS PRETTY OLD-FASHIONED.
PING
GOOD. THIS ISN'T A REMOTE-CONTROL BOMB.

YAN? IS HE THE HEAD OF TEKI?!
SHE FOUND IT.
MAN, THEY'VE GOT SOME SERIOUS ISSUES.
BUT.. HE'S BARELY OLDER THAN ME...
WHAT?!
I'M GLAD I CAUGHT YOU. WE NEED YOUR HELP. WHAT'S THAT?
OH?!
THE REST COMB THE AREA, SEE IF THERE'RE OTHER BOMBS! IF YOU THINK YOU'RE IN REAL DANGER, RUN FOR YOUR LIFE!
Now, move!
GET THE OTHERS OUT OF HERE!
SOME OF YOU STAY TO PUT OUT THE FIRE!
SO IT WASN'T THEIR DOING...
OH!
COPY THAT.
GO! NOW!

THAT NEW EXPLOSIVE, FOX, HAS SUCH AN AWFUL SMELL.
I HOPE THEY PLAN ON FIXING THAT.
It ruined my leather gloves
WHA--?
IT SMELLS FAMILIAR...
WHAT IS IT?
THAT'S RIGHT...
I GOT A WHIFF OF IT THE OTHER DAY ON ONE OF TOYA'S MEN...
ガチン
?!
チョン
...YOU ARE UNDER ARREST.
YAN, HEAD OF TEKI, AND KOTOBUKI...
NEITHER OF YOU MOVE.

I'M CHARGING YOU WITH BURGLARY AND ATTACKS AGAINST THE ARMY THAT GO BEYOND THE BOUNDS OF A RESISTANCE.
TOYA...
WE HAVE ENOUGH EVIDENCE, NOW.
I KNEW YOU WERE UP TO SOMETHING...
BURGLARY? YOU PUT YOUR BOYS UP TO IT!
がばっ
?!
HE PLAYED ME!!
YOU LOST.
Dammit!
YOU'VE HAD...
...THE WHOLE THING PLANNED FROM DAY ONE!!
HE...
I WAS RIGHT. IT'S THE SAME SMELL...

WELL, ENOUGH WHINING.
EMOTION NEVER STAYS STILL. IT CONSTANTLY EVOLVES.
I didn't mean it.
Second generation always gets the short end of the stick.
THIS IS WHY I DIDN'T WANT TO TAKE OVER THE GANG.
BUT I THOUGHT I'D RUN IT MY WAY WITHOUT KNOWING WHAT MY WAY WOULD BE.
Ah
WHY DID I CHANGE MY MIND?
Y-
YAN?
?!
tic
tic
WHAT ARE YOU GOING TO DO WITH YAN?
EVOLVE...
YAN!!
You idiot...
YOU HAVEN'T STOPPED THE BOMB!!

HUH?!
GET RID OF IT...!
AH?!
RAI...!

ARE YOU OKAY?
YEAH, RUNNING ISN'T THAT BAD...
WOW...
LOOKING GOOD, RAIMON.
THEY'RE ALL GONE, SIR!
GO AFTER THEM. YOU MAY USE FORCE, BUT DON'T HURT RAIMON.
LOOK...
HM?
...I'M SORRY...
...I HIT YOU.
THEN KISS ME.
I'M SORRY...

OH.
YOU NEVER KISS ME, KOTOBUKI.
DON'T MIND ME. PRETEND I'M NOT HERE.
Enjoy.
WHA--
Iha ?!
YAN!!
チカッ

……
!!
ザァ
ガク
SHE FELL...
ゴッリ
WE'LL SEARCH FOR KOTOBUKI, JUST IN CASE.
BUT IN THAT POLLUTED WATER, WHAT ARE THE CHANCES...?

THEY THINK IT MIGHT BE BELOW YOUR GROUP'S BASE.
?!
Tsubasa? Seriously?
すっ
TSUBASA.
MANKIND'S DREAM...
I DON'T GET IT. WHY DO YOU WANT TO DESTROY TEKI SO MUCH?
RIGHT, RAIMON?
...TSUBASA HOLDS A SPECIAL MEANING TO THE ARMY. TO US.
WELL DONE. THAT, AND...
RAIMON?

翼を持つ者
つばさ
もの

BEEP
BEEP
NO SIGN OF HER?
NOT YET. BUT IN THAT DIRTY WATER...
...IT'S MOST LIKELY THAT...
...WE'VE LOST HER.
So...
YOU'RE SAYING OUR HOME IS...
...WHERE TSUBASA LANDED.
Heh, heh...
WE DETECTED SOME KIND OF MAGNETIC FIELD RUNNING BELOW HE BUILDING, AND WE BELIEVE IT TO BE TSUBASA.
I had no idea.

IT SOUNDS... COMPLI-CATED.
IS IT REALLY OKAY FOR THE ARMY TO BE DEPENDENT ON TSUBASA?
TSUBASA WILL GIVE US THE POWER TO RUN THE WORLD WITHOUT THE WARS OTHERWISE NEEDED TO ACHIEVE IT.
BUT IF IT FALLS INTO THE HANDS OF OTHER COUNTRIES, IT POSES A REAL THREAT.
IF IT GIVES OUR COUNTRY THE POWER WE ASPIRE TO, YES.
WE'RE WILLING TO TAP INTO IT.
IF WE LAUNCH AN OFFICIAL SEARCH OF THE AREA, OTHER COUNTRIES WILL KNOW WHAT WE'RE UP TO AND DECLARE A WAR.
OF COURSE WE DON'T EXPECT TO FIND TSUBASA ITSELF THERE...
...but there might be a clue.
RIGHT...
SO YOU WENT TO ALL THAT TROUBLE JUST TO DIG UP OUR HOME?
Heh heh...
IT WAS ABSOLUTELY NECESSARY. TSUBASA IS OUR ONLY HOPE.

Heh heh...
YAN, YOU CAN'T POSE A REAL THREAT. YOU JUST DON'T HAVE IT IN YOU.
.....
TAKE HIM TO A CELL.
YOU MAKE IT SOUND LIKE IT'S A WEAPON.
I THOUGHT TSUBASA WAS...
...A MORE HOPEFUL THING.
Oh!
RAIMON, I NEED TO APOLOGIZE...
KOTOBUKI AND I KISSED, ONCE.
SORRY ABOUT THA...
BANG

Come, now...
THAT'S HIS WAY OF SAYING SHUT UP.
Hurry up, or he won't miss next time.
カチッ
DUDE...
YOU'RE DANGEROUS.
Ambidextrous.
ROUND UP THE GROUP. WE'LL MAKE AN EXAMPLE OUT OF YAN IN FRONT OF THEM, AND WE'LL FINISH OFF THE REST LATER.
RAIMON...
THAT WAY, WE CAN FOCUS ON THE DIGGING.
バタン
TOYA.
IF YOU'RE GOING TO EXECUTE YAN SOONER OR LATER...
...WHY NOT JUST MAKE IT TOMORROW AT NOON?
YOU'RE FINALLY...
...BACK WITH US.
OH, SORRY. I COULDN'T RESIST.
No touching the hair.

IT'S NOTHING.
I'M SORRY ABOUT KOTOBUKI.
IT'S...
...FINE.
SO, HOW LONG DID YOU KNOW THAT WE HAD OUR EYES ON TSUBASA?
FROM THE MOMENT I SAW YOU, TOYA.
I'M SO GLAD TO HAVE YOU BACK. WE'LL CONTINUE OUR QUEST FOR TSUBASA LIKE WE USED TO.
HE SEEMS LIKE A DIFFERENT MAN...
THAT'S THE RAIMON I KNOW.
PEOPLE USED TO REGARD HIM IN AWE.
HE CAN BE A HANDFUL, BUT I'M HAPPY TO HAVE HIM BACK ON BOARD.
AT LEAST KOTOBUKI'S DEATH CONTRIBUTED SOMETHING. IT'S NOT LIKE SHE WOULD HAVE EVER ADDED UP TO MUCH ALIVE.

NO... I DON'T WANT TO DIE JUST YET...
I FEEL LIKE I'M BEING SUCKED IN...
SHE WAS TOO BORING...
I WANTED TO PROTECT HIM...
BUT INSTEAD, I HIT HIM...
...I HATE HIM...?
HE WAS SMILING, BUT WHAT IF HE THINKS...
I CAN'T...
WHAT IS...YOUR WISH?
WHAT IS...YOUR WISH ?
...MOVE...
WHAT...?
MY WISH...?

BECAUSE LATELY...
...IT'S BEEN WEIRD.
IT WASN'T LIKE THIS BEFORE.
IS THAT A GOOD OR A BAD THING?
...EVEN THOUGH I MIGHT HURT HIM AGAIN...
WHY?
I WANT TO...
...SEE RAIMON...
YOU'RE EVOLVING FOR SOMEONE YOU CARE ABOUT.
EVOLVING...?
YOU'RE EVOLVING, THAT'S ALL.
"TO LOOK FOR CHANGE MEANS DESTROYING THE PEACE."
SEE?
YES. IT'S NOT DESTROYING. YOU ARE GROWING.
IT'S ALL RIGHT.

LIKE US
THIS IS EVOLUTION.
NOW YOU WILL GET YOUR WISH.
THE REST IS UP TO YOU...
IT'S GLOWING IN THIS POLLUTED WATER...
IT'S SO... BEAUTIFUL...

IT'S A LOVELY DAY FOR EXECUTION, ISN'T IT?
YAN!!
YOU SAID YOU WOULDN'T KILL HIM IF WE TURNED OURSELVES IN!!
YAN!!
I look lame.
DON'T WORRY. THEY'LL BE FOLLOWING YOU.
Huh?
FIRST THE GIRL, AND NOW MY YS? I FEEL ORTHLESS.
DON'T MAKE IT ANY HARDER FOR ME.
SORRY, GUYS. THEY USED ME AS BAIT...
I'VE NEVER FELT SO STUPID.

SO DO THE WORLD A FAVOR...
...AND FINISH ME OFF.
?!
Ugh...
I GOT SEAWATER ON ME...
...YOU...?
JUST GET IT OVER WITH, WHY DON'T...

W-wha--?!
SHE'S NOT DEAD?!
Yan...?
WHAT'S GOING ON?
YOU LOOK LIKE A PRISONER WAITING...
UH...
.....
...TO BE EXECUT-ED...
Gyah?!
SOLDIERS...

BACK OFF!!
WHY ARE YOU EXECUTING HIM?!
RAIMON...
YOU GOT IT.
THERE YOU ARE. THEY SHOULD BE DONE WITH THE EXECUTION BY NOW.
GATHER EVERYONE UP. WE HAVE SOME EXPLAINING TO DO.

HOW DID YOU GET OUT OF THE WATER?
Huh?
Yan!
I-I JUST DID...
YOU TELL ME. ARE YOU OKAY? YOU DON'T FEEL SICK?
Huff
Huff
Thank goodness!
Yan!
THAT WAS CLOSE...
YOU OKAY, YAN?
I HEARD A VOICE...
Wow.
ABOVE AND BEYOND?
Oh.
HE'S BACK IN THE ARMY.
Yan!
HUH?
RAIMON!
WHERE IS HE?!
IT WAS SO BEAUTIFUL... IT ASKED ME WHAT I WANTED...
UH... HE SEEMED FINE WITH IT, TO ME...
TOYA FORCED HIM TO RETURN, RIGHT?!

Yaan
ALTHOUGH HE'S DIFFERENT, NOW. HE'S SCARY...
NO... I CAN'T BELIEVE HE'D DO THAT...
SOMETHING MUST HAVE HAPPENED WHEN I WAS GONE!!
!
...PROTECT RAIMON, DON'T I?!
I'VE GOT TO SAVE RAIMON...!
Ugh!
QUIT WHINING. I'VE FORGOTTEN SOMETHING...
I WANT TO...
HOW?
BUT I WILL GET HIM OUT OF THERE.
NOT YET...
Uh...
GOT ANY PLANS?
Now freed.

I DON'T KNOW IF HE GOT OVER IT.
I'VE GOT TO SEE HIM...
WITH THE POWER OF LOVE!!
?
NOT THAT I'D EVER REALLY SAY THAT...
I'LL HELP YOU OUT.
...AND TELL HIM THAT I LIKE HIM.
OH?
...MAKES ME WANT TO TAKE MY CHANCES WITH YOU.
YOU SAVED MY LIFE, AFTER ALL.
AND THE WAY YOU SHOWED UP WHEN EVERYONE THOUGHT YOU WERE DEAD...
.....?

...OUR HIDE-OUT!!
GIVE ME A BREAK.
Whoa!
ANOTHER EXPLOSION?!
IT'S NOT FROM TOWN. IT'S...
THE ROCKY HILL FELL BECAUSE OF THE EXPLOSION.
MAJOR, THE DOOR IS BLOCKED.
OH, DEAR... HOW'D THAT HAPPEN?
RAIMON, ARE YOU OKAY?

RAIMON...
THAT WAS JUST A TEST. I SET DOZENS OF BOMBS IN THE MOUNTAIN. THEY'LL GO OFF IN FIVE MINUTES.
THIS HILL IS NOT VERY BIG.
IT WAS YOU...
I DON'T WANT TO DIE ALONE...
...ARE GOING TO SINK INTO THE SEA WITH ME.
...SO YOU AND TSUBASA...
No.
I DON'T THINK HE IS.
HE'S BLUFFING, RIGHT?
DON'T MOVE.

WHEN ASKED WHY HE DID IT, HE SAID HE WAS BORED.
HE'S DONE THIS TWICE IN THE PAST.
THE FIRST TIME, HE AND SEVERAL OTHER OFFICERS WERE BADLY HURT.
ごく……
WHY ARE YOU DOING THIS...?
I DON'T WANT TO LIVE IF KOTOBUKI...
...ISN'T HERE.
SHE WAS ALWAYS SO FULL OF HOPE.
I TOLD YOU... KOTOBUKI WAS STILL IN THE MAKING.
SHE WAS GROWING.
KOTOBUKI?!
WHAT'S SO SPECIAL ABOUT HER?!

MAJOR!!
YOU RUINED IT...
...TOYA.
SHE WAS THE ONLY THING...
...THAT GAVE MEANING TO MY LIFE...
YOU...
YA!!
.....
I TOLD YOU NOT TO MOVE...
...DIDN'T I?

HE CAN'T BE... STOPPED.
I'M JUST SAD THAT YOU'VE BETRAYED ME.
CAT GOT YOUR TONGUE, TOYA?
WHAT'S WRONG? ARE YOU AFRAID?
Heh...
...STUPID.
THIS IS THE REAL RAIMON.
ONCE HE SNAPS, THERE'S NO STOPPING HIM.
THERE'S NO ONE...
OUCH...

KOTOBUKI ...?
?!
RAIMON, YOU'RE BLEEDING...!
Stop...!
DON'T! HE'S DANGERO--
WHAT'S UP WITH YOU, RAIMON...?
THERE YOU ARE...
.....

ドキン
I LIKE HIM.
.....!
...YEAH.
I'M SORRY I MESSED UP... WERE YOU...
...WORRIED?
JUST BEING... CLOSE TO HIM...
THAT'S HOW MUCH I LIKE HIM.
...IS NOT ENOUGH ANYMORE.
I LIKE HIM. I LIKE HIM SO MUCH.
I CAN SAY IT A HUNDRED TIMES OVER, BUT IT STILL WON'T BE ENOUGH.

I WAS GOING THROUGH AN EVOLUTION.
...THAT I STARTED TO LIKE HIM...
IT TOOK ME A WHILE TO REALIZE...
THIS IS A FIRST...
...A LOT MORE THAN BEFORE.
RIGHT?
ひょい!っ
WHOA!
STOP THAT! YOU'RE SCARING ME.
AH HA HA!
YOU KISSED ME.

YOU COULDN'T STAND BEING TOUCHED BY ME...
...BUT YOU'RE FINE WITH HER...
KOTOBUKI...
IT'S REALLY YOU...
YOU'RE NOT DEAD...
I'M GLAD I'VE NOTICED HIM.
BECAUSE IT...
...FEELS SO GOOD.
WE SHOULD GET OUT OF HERE...
...BEFORE THE BOMBS GO OFF.
OH!
Huh?

LET'S RUN.
SO WHAT HAPPENED TO COMMITTING SUICIDE, RAIMON?
That's sudden.
LET'S GO... OH, AND YAN IS OUTSIDE.
NOW...
Huh?
WHAT SUICIDE?
WHAAAT?!
YAN!
THERE SHE IS...
RUN!!
THE CLIFF'S GONNA COLLAPSE!
Phew...
KOTOBUKI CLIMBED UP THE WINDOW AND TOOK OFF.
I HOPE SHE'S OKAY.

ドドド

HAVE A CLOSER LOOK, KOTOBUKI.
THE WATER RUNNING OVER IT IS CLEAR.
MAYBE IT'S SEA ANEMONE...?
OH....
I SAW THAT IN THE WATER...!!
HMM...
.....
YEAH... IT IS.
NOW WE KNOW HOW YOU GOT OUT OF THE WATER FINE.
I GUESS IT EVOLVED...
THAT WASN'T HERE BEFORE.
IT'S CLEANING THE POLLUTED WATER OF THE SEA.

...
KOTOBUKI.
SO IT'S ALL RIGHT...
...TO TAKE YOUR TIME, TOO...
IN THE POLLUTED WATER...
...IT GREW UP LITTLE BY LITTLE...
...RAIMON KNEW EVERYTHING...
IT SEEMS LIKE...
"LIKE US."
...THE WHOLE TIME.
HEY...
UH... WHAT'S THAT?
HM?

?!
ばあっ
YOUR WISH...
THAT VOICE...!!
...CAME TRUE.
WHAT...
...WAS THAT...?
I'M VERY HAPPY FOR YOU.
.....
THAT'S GOOD.

YOU'VE GOTTA BE JOKING! I WANNA SEE IT AGAIN!
IT FLEW AWAY.
"WHAT IS..."
"...YOUR WISH?"
TSUBASA?
COULD IT BE...
"WHAT IS YOUR WISH?"
IT'S POSSIBLE.
WHAAT?!
I...
I'M NOT SURE. BUT IT SAID SOMETHING ABOUT A WISH...
...AND RAIMON FELL OFF THE RADAR AGAIN.
The colonel won't be pleased...
WE LOST TEKI, TSUBASA IS AT THE BOTTOM OF THE OCEAN...
OH, DEAR...

SHE HAS... POTENTIAL.
AT LEAST SHE STOPPED RAIMON...
KOTOBUKI HAS...
KOTOBUKI WON THIS TIME.
WE CAN SEND OUR FORCE...
NO, I'LL GIVE UP FOR NOW.
Until then... I'll keep my diaries.
What diaries?
I'M SURE WE'LL SEE EACH OTHER AGAIN.
IT WAS SO BEAUTIFUL...
IF A DREAM COULD HAVE A SHAPE, IT WOULD BE THAT.
NO WAY! I'D RATHER NOT SEE HIM AGAIN.
SO, IN A NUT-SHELL...
...TSUBASA SAVED YOUR LIFE. TOYA WOULD BE HAPPY TO HEAR THAT.
He might experiment on your body.

HE KNOWS!!
I-I'M SO SORRY!
IT WAS AN ACCIDENT! I KNOW THIS SOUNDS LAME, BUT...
YEP. HE KISSED YOU.
RAIMON...
DID YOU REALLY TRY TO KILL HIM?
UM...
I'LL FORGIVE YOU IF YOU KISS ME. ♡
ぴたっ
...IS SO BIG.
THE ARMY, TSUBASA, BORDERS...
Heh heh...
...I'LL HAVE TO WAIT A BIT LONGER TO MAKE YOU A WOMAN.
THE WORLD...
じーん
WHY ARE YOU ALWAYS LIKE THAT?
KOZO

HUH?
It's just...
YOU MADE ME REALIZE THAT I NEED TO SEE MORE OF THE WORLD.
I NEED THAT TO KEEP RUNNING THE RESISTANCE...
I'M GLAD...
...THAT THERE'S STILL SOMEONE LIKE YOU.
THE WORLD IS FULL OF THINGS WAITING TO BE DISCOVERED.
HE ALMOST KILLED ME, YOU KNOW.
I'M GONNA GO. HAVE FUN WITH YOUR BOYFRIEND.
I can hear you.
HE'S A DISASTER WAITING TO HAPPEN, AND YOU'RE THE ONLY ONE WHO CAN STOP HIM.
YAN!
YO!
WHAT?!
HOPE TO SEE YOU AGAIN.
Bye!

...YOU CAN EVOLVE.
BUT...
YANK
...AND RAIMON...
SOMETIMES EVERYTHING SEEMS OVERWHELMING FOR ME, BUT--
Twirl
...LITTLE BY LITTLE...
IT WAS FUN WATCHING YOU GET UPSET, THOUGH. ♡
YOU ARE SUCH A PIECE OF WORK.
ONE KISS...
...A DAY.

NOT GONNA HAPPEN. THIS IS MY TREASURE YOU'RE TALKING ABOUT. IT'S PROOF OF MY LOVE. NOW YOU KNOW HOW I FEEL ABOUT YOU, RAIMON.
Oh, no!!
YOU WILL NEVER GET MARRIED...
Stay away.
I'M NOT THAT KEEN ON THE PHOTOS.
TOYA, FANS WANT TO SEE YOUR PHOTO COLLECTION OF RAIMON.
HM?
NO WAY!!
A secret revealed!!
HE'S GOT A WIFE AND KIDS.
WHAT? IS SOMETHING WRONG?

翼を持つ者

!!
FANS WANT TO SEE SOME ACTION BETWEEN RAIMON AND KOTOBUKI. SOME EVEN THINK RAIMON SHOULD THROW HIMSELF AT KOTOBUKI. ANY COMMENTS, GUYS?

AT LEAST THE READERS HAVE SOMETHING TO LOOK FORWARD TO.
DON'T SAY ANOTHER WORD...
じー
Don't stare...
WHEN IT HAPPENS, IT HAPPENS.
You seem ready.

WELL... MY PRIORITY IS KOTOBUKI, SO I DON'T WANT TO RUSH AND HURT HER FEELINGS.
IF I FORCE MYSELF ON HER, I'LL HURT HER FEELINGS. AND HAVING A RELATIONSHIP IS NOT ALL ABOUT SEX. BUT LET ME ASSURE YOU...

THINKING THAT IS BAD LUCK!!
And with a sigh.
WHETHER OR NOT THERE'S MORE...
Sigh...
...is beyond our control.

Four Seasons
"...LIFE."
THIEF!!
YOU LITTLE DIRTBAG!! YOU ARE A NAMELESS ONE, AREN'T YOU?!
THE NAMELESS ONES ARE BETTER OFF DEAD!!
"GOOD LUCK TO ALL OF US."
"LET'S FIND OUR PROOF OF..."

THERE WERE SO MANY WARS. THE FIELDS ARE WITHERED, AND ORDINARY PEOPLE SUFFER IN POVERTY.
IT'S THE END OF THE 22ND CENTURY ON EARTH.
BUT LIFE GOES ON, NO MATTER WHAT.
IT'S NICE OUT.
THAT'S GOOD.
I'M KOTOBUKI. I USED TO BE A THIEF IN ORDER TO SURVIVE THE HARD TIMES...

Morning!
LET'S WORK HARD, TODAY.
Yaay!
I GOT A JOB AT AN ORPHANAGE.
...BUT THAT'S ALL BEHIND ME, NOW.
I'VE BEEN TRAVELING FROM TOWN TO TOWN TO FIND AN HONEST JOB...
OH!
...AND I FINALLY DID IT.
GOOD MORNING KOTOBUKI
KOTOBUKI.
Oh!
GOOD MORNING, DIRECTOR.
THE ORPHANAGE IS BUILT OUT OF A ROCKY MOUNTAIN.
I DO A LITTLE BIT OF EVERYTHING THERE.

Don't be silly!
THIS IS MY CALLING.
THANK YOU FOR YOUR HARD WORK...
EVEN THOUGH WE'RE NOT PAYING YOU MUCH...
HAVE YOU SEEN RAIMON?
RAIMON?
HE WAS CLEANING UP THE LOUNGE.
OH.
I ALMOST FORGOT.
Now...
TIME FOR LAUNDRY AND TIDYING-UP! I'LL GET THE WATER AND THEN I'LL COOK.
WHAT AN ENERGETIC CHILD...
It's as if she's sucking up my energy.
I'LL HELP YOU OUT.

W-WHAT'S GOING ON? WHAT ARE YOU DOING?!
And what's up with the broom?
I'M CLEANING.
W-WHY? WHAT FOR?
GOOD MORNING. ♡
RAIMON IS CLEANING UP?!
RAIMON!!
RAIMON WAS A YOUNG CAPTAIN WITH A BRIGHT FUTURE...
...BUT HE QUIT THE ARMY BECAUSE HE WANTED TO BE WITH ME.
I JUST WANTED T HELP YOU KOTOBUKI
TAP
THIS IS MY COMPANION, RAIMON SHIRAGI.

Hee!
Yay!
COME ON, GUYS. WE SHOULD KEEP THOSE LOVEBIRDS ALONE.
Kotabuki!
WE'VE BEEN TRAVELING TOGETHER EVER SINCE.
WE'LL DO THE LAUNDRY.
HUH? WAIT!!
ばしゅうぅ
GOOD BOY.
Help needed at orphanage
WHEN I WAS A MAID, HE DIDN'T EVEN RAISE A FINGER.
BUT...
...RAIMON...
YOU DON'T HAVE TO GO TO THE TROUBLE TO DO ALL THIS...
GO AHEAD.
IT'S DIFFERENT THIS TIME.
THERE'S AN OPENING AT AN ORPHANAGE... I WANT TO CHECK IT OUT.

DON'T WORRY ABOUT ME. THIS IS A DREAM COME TRUE FOR YOU.
...YEAH.
MY DREAM WAS TO FIND WORK.
ALTHOUGH HE LOOKS QUITE COMFORTABLE AROUND KIDS...
Oddly enough...
THE RAIMON I KNOW DOESN'T CARE ABOUT ANYONE AND TREATS EVERYONE LIKE DIRT.
I'VE NEVER SEEN THIS SIDE OF HIM.
I'LL START WORKING, TOO.
smooch
GOOD LUCK.
I WANTED TO QUIT ROBBING AND START A NEW LIFE. I WANTED TO STAND ON MY OWN TWO FEET.
THEN I'LL BELIEVE IN MYSELF.

IT'S A STEP TOWARDS BECOMING MORE LIKE SOMEONE WORTHY OF HIS ATTENTION.
Meow...
mumble...
MY ONLY CONCERN IS THAT HIS SECOND HOUSE IS IN THIS TOWN...
ベ
ベ
MYA?
AND THERE'S THIS GUY...
OH!
IT'S NOTHING. ♡
WHAT'S WRONG?
WE WENT TO TOWN FOR SHOPPING...
SIS KOTOBUKI!
SOMEBODY PLEASE HELP!!

HEY!!
STOP THAT! HE'S ONLY A CHILD!!

HERE.
YOU WANT IT, YOU TAKE IT.

MOMMY, WHAT IS A NAMELESS ONE?

ぴく

だ
KOTOBUKI ...!
WHO ARE YOU?
A FRIEND OF THOSE NAMELESS ONES?

IF YOU DON'T HAVE A NAME, THEY WON'T ISSUE YOU IDENTIFICATION. THAT'S WHY THEY'RE CALLED NAMELESS ONES.
IT'S PEOPLE WHO DON'T HAVE A FAMILY. YOU BECOME A NAMELESS ONE...
...IF YOUR PARENTS DIE OR ABANDON YOU.
OH, REALLY? THEN WE WANT OUR MONEY BACK.
WELL, THE PRICES ARE SOARING.
YOU CAN'T EVEN BUY ONE BLOCK OF SUGAR.
OH, YOU'RE THE WOMAN WHO'S STARTED WORKING IN THAT DUMP.
LET THEM EAT ROOTS. KEEPS THEM IN THEIR PLACE.
Ah ha ha!
Idiot.
THIS MONEY CAME FROM THE ARMY, RIGHT?
THEN IT'S OUR MONEY. WE PAY TAXES.
IT'S CALLED AN ORPHANAGE.
IT'S NOT A WISE DECISION...

YOU WANT IT BACK?
ポーン
THEN COME AND GET IT!
AGH!
I GOT IT!
Bitch...
WHAT THE-- GIVE THAT BACK TO ME!
YOU TOLD ME TO GET IT, SO I DID...
YOU LITTLE...

KOTOBUKI!!
!
YOU'RE DEAD, YOU SCUM.
SNAP
GAAAHHH!
NO VIOLENCE, PLEASE.
LET'S TALK.
YOU...!!
LET'S NOT GET ROUGH...
...on such a sweet lady.
RAIMON...
You took your time walking here.

SEE?
VIOLENCE BRINGS YOU NOTHING.
.....

WHAT WAS THAT SOUND?!
?!
.....
Corpu!
YOU DIDN'T HAVE TO DO THAT...
I NEED SOME GOOD EXERCISE.
.....
Stupid!
THEY STILL WANT YOU BACK.
THEY'VE MADE THAT ABUNDANTLY CLEAR, REMEMBER?
THE ARMY HAS UNFINISHED BUSINESS WITH RAIMON.
IT'LL BE FINE.
Thanks for caring. ♡
THOUGH I DON'T KNOW WHAT MAKES HIM SO VALUABLE TO THEM.
Oh, no!
IT'S THE ARMY AGAIN!!
RAIMON, WE'D BETTER RUN.
WHY?

HE'S OUT OF IT. DID YOU HIT HIM?!
Huh?
THAT'S JUST STUPID.
OF COURSE I DIDN'T HIT HIM.
I KICKED HIM.
YOU IDIOT!!
HEY...
NICE GUN.
A CONVERTED GUN MANU-FACTURED BY CORPUL CORP.
It's his. Not mine.
WHA--

LET'S GO.
EH?!
But--
WE'RE FREE TO WALK.
...LET'S GET YOU HOME.
"NAMELESS ONE"!!
ギゅっ
WHAT'S THE PROBLEM?
OH, SIR, IT'S--
SIR, WE HAVE A SITUATION...
I SEE...

...OKAY.
TO TELL YOU THE TRUTH, IT'S NOT THE FIRST TIME WE'VE BEEN TREATED THAT WAY...
OF COURSE, THE ARMY HELPS US FINANCIALLY...
...BUT THEY DON'T GIVE US MUCH.
FOR NOW, GIV THE POOR GL SOME TIME T COOL OFF.
The poor guy.
YES, SIR...
カチ
...OH, DEAR.
WHO WOULD KNOW SOMETHING LIKE THAT...
...OTHER THAN HIM?

THANKS TO ROSS'S HELP...
...WE MANAGE WELL.
ROSS WHO?
THERE HAS BEEN A STRING OF ATTACKS AGAINST ORPHANAGES. SOMEONE'S ON A DESTROYING SPREE.
I HAVE ONE WORRY, THOUGH.
HE HAS A LARGE SECOND HOUSE IN THIS TOWN.
A WEALTHY MAN WHO HAS BEEN SPONSORING US FOR DECADES.
BUT WHY ORPHAN-AGES?
WHAT?! WHY?!
I DON'T THINK THEY'RE TARGETING US... IT'S JUST A WAY OF GETTING AT AUTHORITIES LIKE THE ARMY.
I DON'T KNOW.
PERHAPS THEY ARE WHAT YOU CALL BLUE ROSE.
Here's an article.

CAN I SEE THE ARTICLE?
OH... SURE.
SOME CHILDREN CAN'T EVEN GET INTO AN ORPHANAGE.
THE POOR CHILDREN. WHY DO THEY HAVE TO GO THROUGH SUCH MISERY?
NO FAMILY NAME, NO MEANS OF IDENTIFICATION... AND NO CHANCE AT EDUCATION.
DO YOU WANT A LOOK, TOO KOTOBUKI?
I CAN'T READ IT.
I can only write and read a few basic words.
.....
...THANKS, BUT...
TO TELL YOU THE TRUTH...
I'M A NAMELESS, TOO.

WE CAN DO THIS.
I REALLY ADMIRE WHAT YOU DO, LADY, TAKING CARE OF ALL THOSE KIDS BY YOURSELF.
...OH MY.
WE'RE IN THIS TOGETHER.
LET'S LIVE!
OH...!!
THREE BLOWN UP BUILDINGS... A FEW DEAD BODIES...
Anyway,
THIS IS A PRETTY BIG CASE.
YES, SURE...
THAT'S A GOOD IDEA.

I HATE HIM WITH A PASSION!!
TOYA?
Who?
HOW CAN THE ARMY LET THEM COMMIT SUCH HORRIBLE ACTS AND NOT DO ANYTHING?
WHAT IS TOYA DOING, ANYWAY?!
はくしょん
Sneeze
...DO YOU HAPPEN TO HATE HIM?
Such negative vibes.
YOUR FORMER SUPERIOR WHO HA A COLLECTION OF YOUR PHOTOS AND IS KEEPING DIARIES ABOUT YOU. DOES THE NAME MAJOR TOYA INGRAM RING A BELL?
Previously on Tsubasa: Toya tricked Kotobuki and almost caused her to get killed.
(In Japan, it's said that when you sneeze, there's someone's talking about you somewhere.)
DID YOU CATCH A COLD MAJOR INGRAM
MAYBE RAIMON'S TALKING ABOUT ME.
GOOD.
GO AHEAD WITH THE ASSIGNMENT, LIEUTENANT MARSHEL.
ANY PROGRESS ON THE ORPHANAGE BOMBING CASE...?
IN OUR FAVOR, SIR

THERE'S SO MANY...
..PROBLEMS VE HAVE TO EAL WITH...
YOU THINK SO?
WE RUN.
I'd rather not, but if it comes to it...
WE GO DUE ORTH, WE'LL OME ACROSS HE BORDER.
NOW THAT'S A PROBLEM.
WELL, YEAH. LIKE YOURS.
I HOPE THE OFFICER FROM THIS AFTERNOON DIDN'T RECOGNIZE YOU.
WHAT IF HE DID?
Not many common officers know me.
YES, SIR.

ACTUALLY, THERE REALLY IS A PROBLEM.

FORGET IT.
THERE IS A BOMB INSIDE MY BODY SET TO GO OFF THE MOMENT I CROSS THE BORDER. YES, I AM A ROBOT.

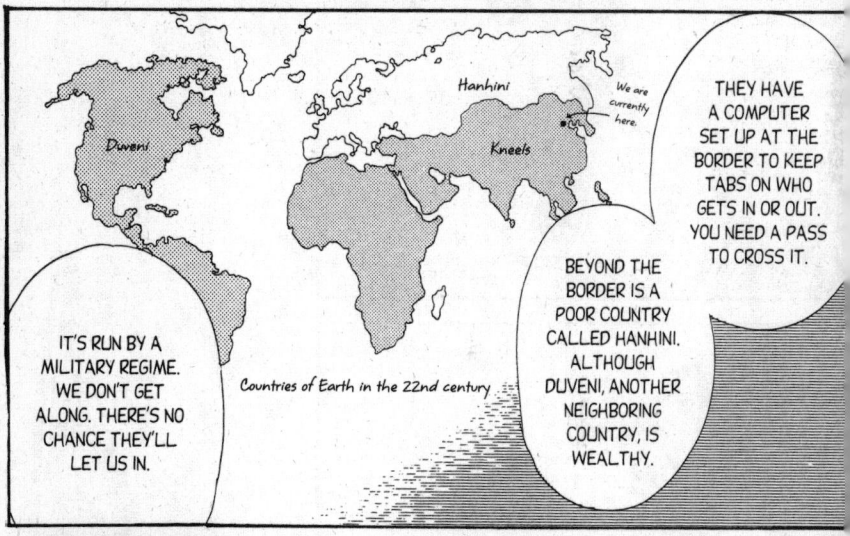
Hanhini
We are currently here.
Kneels
Duveni
Countries of Earth in the 22nd century
THEY HAVE A COMPUTER SET UP AT THE BORDER TO KEEP TABS ON WHO GETS IN OR OUT. YOU NEED A PASS TO CROSS IT.
BEYOND THE BORDER IS A POOR COUNTRY CALLED HANHINI. ALTHOUGH DUVENI, ANOTHER NEIGHBORING COUNTRY, IS WEALTHY.
IT'S RUN BY A MILITARY REGIME. WE DON'T GET ALONG. THERE'S NO CHANCE THEY'LL LET US IN.

.....
RAIMON KNOWS EVERYTHING!!

YOU DON'T KNOW WHAT COULD SPARK A WAR.
DON'T WORRY. IT WON'T HAPPEN THAT EASILY.
A WAR?!

...RAIMON. DID YOU KNOW I WAS A NAMELESS ONE?
WHAT DO YOU THINK OF NAMELESS ONES?
OF COURSE HE CAN READ. HE USED TO BE IN THE ARMY.
WHETHER YOU'RE A NAMELESS ONE OR AN OFFICER... TITLES MEAN NOTHING TO ME.
DON'T GIVE A DAMN IF PEOPLE ARE DYING IN THE STREETS OR WHATEVER.
IT'S THE PLACE FOR THE PRIVILEGED FEW.
HOWEVER...
...I'D NEVER WANT TO MAKE YOU SAD, KOTOBUKI.
.....
HOW'S THAT FOR AN ANSWER?

THANKS...
I CAN'T HELP IT
I'VE BUILT MY WORLD AROUND YOU, KOTOBUKI.
.....
THAT'S SO YOU, RAIMON.

...IT'S TIME TO GO ALL THE WAY?
Phew...
YOU STOPPED RUNNING AWAY WHEN I KISS.
ポー
DOES THAT MEAN...
?
Aww...
DON'T BE AFRAID.
There, there.
I'M NOT AN ANIMAL TO BE HANDLED!!
Put me down!
NO WAY!!
Nooo!
カミャマー
DON'T WORRY. I'LL BE GENTLE.
I've been waiting for so long.

GET LOST, NAMELESS ONES!!
NEXT TIME, IT'LL BE MUCH BIGGER THAN A STONE!
!
WHAT'S THAT?!
EAT THIS!!
?!
.....!!
.....
HOW AWFUL...

WHY DOES EVERYBODY TREAT THE NAMELESS ONES LIKE TRASH?
STAY WHERE YOU ARE!!
I'LL SMASH YOUR SKULL IN!!
WERE WE BROUGHT TO THE WORLD ONLY TO BE DESPISED?
KOTOBUKI...
ARE WE BORN WORTHLESS?
I'VE BEEN THINKING...

Dammit!
I'M GOING TO REPORT THIS TO THE FORCES!!
WE LOST THEM.

ARE NAMELESS ONES REALLY WORTHLESS?

BUT...IF WE LET THEM GO, THEY'LL COME BACK AND DESTROY THE ORPHANAGE...
WAIT!! THERE'S ROSS!!
DON'T WASTE YOUR TIME. YOU WON'T GET THEIR ATTENTION.

Wait, wait.
KOTOBUKI--

HE'S THE SPONSOR AND HE'S NOT FROM THE ARMY, RIGHT?
MAYBE HE CAN HELP US. LET ME AT HIM!

IT'S HUGE...
IS THIS REALLY HIS HOUSE?
BOLTING OUT WITHOUT AN ADDRESS WAS STUPID...
...but this is the largest house around.
Beep
Beep

DONG
?!
IT'S OPENING...
GOOD EVENING.
Oh...
HELLO... UM..
YOU'RE HERE FOR ROSS?

.....?
IS HE A SERVANT...? OR MAYBE A SON?
What weird clothes...
Ah!
YES! I AM!
I'LL TAKE YOU.
COME THIS WAY.
W--
WOW...
.....!
ALL THE LIGHTS ARE ON... IT LOOKS EXPENSIVE...

OF ALL THE HOUSES I BROKE INTO, THERE WAS NOTHING LIKE THIS...
WE'RE HERE.
OH.
THANKS...
I KNOW YOU...
I'VE KNOWN YOU...
...FOR A LONG TIME.
KOTOBUKI.

I'M SO GLAD...
...WE GOT TO MEET AGAIN...
HE...
...VANISHED INTO THIN AIR!!
Weeeek!!
OH...
WHO WAS THAT?!
WHAT'S GOING ON? WHAT IS HE?!

I-I'VE COME TO SEE ROSS.
まずい
まず
WHAT? HOW DID YOU GET IN?!
ROSS?
WHAT'S GOING ON?
THAT WOULD BE ME.
was sleeping
ARE YOU REALLY ROSS?
Yawn...
THAT'S RIGHT. WELL, WELL. I'M FLATTERED...
...THAT SUCH A LOVELY YOUNG LADY CAME ALL THE WAY HERE JUST TO SEE ME.
Let's go to bed!
YOU'RE WRONG!!

I CAN'T STAND NAMELESS ONES.
STOP.
SOMEONE ATTACKED THE PLACE, AND I--
YES, I'VE BEEN THROWING IN AN ARM AND A LEG. BUT THAT'S ALL THERE IS TO IT. I CAN'T HELP YOU.
I WORK IN THE ORPHANAGE YOU SPONSOR.
OH, REALLY?
And?
IF YOU TRULY INSIST, I'LL LISTEN TO WHAT YOU HAVE TO SAY...
THEN... WHY...
...IN BED. ♪
YOU OLD GOAT...

OWW...
!!
RAIMON...
How did you get in?
DO YOU KNOW EACH OTHER, RAIMON?
Wow!
YOU'RE HIS GIRLFRIEND!
?!
ザワ....
Master Raimon?
Master Raimon?
IS THIS HOW YOU TREAT ME AFTER ALL THOSE YEARS?
I KNEW IT WAS YOU.
YOU'RE AS STUPID AS EVER, ROSS.

LET ME INTRODUCE MYSELF, MY DEAR. I AM...
...RAIMON'S DAD! ♡
D--
IT'S NICE TO MEET YOU. ♡
DAAAD?!
Make us tea.
I will if you call me dad.

翼を持つ者

YEAH... RAIMON'S A HUMAN AFTER ALL.
...BUT ACTUALLY SEEING THEM IS SOMETHING ELSE.
OF COURSE HE HAS PARENTS...
Well, well.
MAKE YOURSELF AT HOME, KOTOBUKI. MORE TEA?
OKAY...
I STILL CAN'T BELIEVE HE HAS A DAD!!
Here.
He changed clothes.

...
Heh...
LIFE IN THE COUNTRY DOESN'T SEEM TO AGREE WITH HER. SHE'S BACK HOME.
AND A WEALTHY AND PRETTY (?) DAD, AT THAT.
RAIMON REALLY IS A PRODUCT OF THE UPPER-CLASS BACKGROUND...
WHERE'S MOTHER?

ANYWAY, IT'S BEEN A WHILE, HASN'T IT?
YOU DIDN'T TELL ME ABOUT LEAVING THE ARMY. YOU JUST UP AND WALKED AWAY WITHOUT A WORD.
I SUPPOSE KOTOBUKI WAS THE DRIVING FORCE BEHIND THAT.

カッ!!
MOTHER?!
I WANT TO SEE RAIMON'S MOM!!
?

JUST LET HER TALK, WILL YOU?
Ooh...
YOU'RE LOVELY. AND THAT SKIN... IT LOOKS SO SOFT! ♡

HE'S LAID-BACK, TOO, BUT NOT QUITE LIKE RAIMON...
I WORK AT THE ORPHANAGE THAT YOU SPONSOR... RAIMON DOES, TOO.
SOME PEOPLE ARE GIVING US A HARD TIME.
THERE'S BEEN A SERIES OF ATTACKS TARGETING ORPHANAGES, AND WE'RE ALL WORRIED.
I WAS HOPING MAYBE YOU COULD HELP US P--
I HATE TO REPEAT MYSELF, BUT...
I CAN'T STAND NAMELESS ONES.
I DON'T WANT ANY PART OF IT.
.....
THEN WHY ARE YOU HELPING THEM?
I HAD NO CHOICE. IT WAS SOMETHING MY GRANDFATHER DID.
WHY...?

SO IS THAT IT?
WE'RE BORN SIMPLY TO BE DESPISED?
WHY DO YOU HATE NAMELESS ONES SO MUCH...?!
WHAT DID WE DO TO MAKE EVERYONE HATE US?
THEY'RE DISGUSTING.
THEY HAVE NO EDUCATION OR MANNERS.
THE NAMELESS THIEF KOTOBUKI.
THEY'RE ALSO THE FIRST ONES TO COMMIT A CRIME.
BUT I GUESS YOU KNOW THAT VERY WELL.

I'M LEAVING...
I'M NOT PICKY WHEN IT COMES TO A BED PARTNER. ♡
I HOPE YOU STAY LONGER NEXT TIME.
クス
Shh. They can hear us.
クス
DID YOU HEAR THAT? SERIOUSLY?
HOW COME RAIMON LIKES HER?
Heh...
TALK ABOUT BAD TASTE.
カン!
IN YOUR DREAMS!!
DID YOU KNOW THAT IT'S OFTEN THE EDUCATED PEOPLE...
...WHO HAVE NO BRAINS OR CLASS?
IMAGINE HOW SURPRISED I WAS WHEN TOYA TOLD ME ABOUT HER.
LOOK...

ARE YOU WORRIED ABOUT SOMETHING?
IS THAT...
... A WARNING?
Not really.
WHO SAID I WAS TALKING ABOUT YOU?
MY ADVICE TO THEM WOULD BE...
...TO START WORRYING BEFORE SOMEONE STABS THEM IN THE BACK.
ぱたん
Ha ha ha...
OH DEAR. PARDON MY FRENCH.
IT JUST CAME OUT.
GET ME A PHONE, WILL YOU?
...YOU DAMNED BRAT.

"DISGUSTING."
THAT HASN'T BEEN THE FIRST TIME SOMEONE INSULTED US...
...BUT THE FACT THAT IT WAS RAIMON'S DAD MAKES ALL THE DIFFERENCE...
OF COURSE, NO FATHER WOULD WANT...
...HIS SON TO BE WITH A NAMELESS THIEF...
KOTOBUKI.
I HAVE TO...
...CALL MAJOR INGRAM.
I GUESS I GOT LOST.
It's so big.
?
OW DID YOU FIND YOUR AY TO HIS ROOM?
YOU'RE GOING THE WRONG WAY.
HM? OH!!

"I'M SO GLAD WE GOT TO MEET AGAIN."
Oh yeah!!
HE JUST VANISHED!
I DON'T REALLY KNOW...
?
THERE WAS THIS STRANGE BOY WHO LET ME IN...
HOW...?
WAS HE A GHOST, OR WAS IT A DREAM?
"I KNOW YOU."
"I'VE KNOWN YOU FOR A LONG TIME..."
"...KOTOBUKI."
HE DIDN'T LOOK FAMILIAR, BUT IT'S POSSIBLE I'VE FORGOTTEN...

WE'VE NEVER GOTTEN ALONG. EVER.
IT'S FINE. I'M MORE WORRIED ABOUT YOU. IS EVERYTHING OKAY BETWEEN YOU TWO?
OH, THAT. I DON'T CARE.
KOTOBUKI.
I'M SORRY ABOUT WHAT HAPPENED BACK THERE.
EH?!
DON'T LET HIS WORDS GET TO YOU.
WHOA!!
YOU'RE DOING GREAT.
YOU'VE BEEN DOING GREAT.

DON'T WORRY. I'LL BE FINE.
...MAKE ME FEEL SO MUCH BETTER.
HIS WORDS...
LET'S GO HOME.
...IT'S JUST THAT...
SINCE I CAN'T TURN TO YOUR DAD, I'M GOING TO TAKE THE MATTER INTO MY HANDS!
HIS UNRELIABILITY HAS NEVER BEEN IN DOUBT.
IT'S JUST...
ANYWAY!
DOES MY PRESENCE EVER EMBARRASS HIM?
THAT THOUGHT...

AS FOR...
...BREAKS MY HEART.
THERE WAS A CALL FROM ROSS.
RAIMON SHOWED UP AT HIS DOOR.
HE SAID HE'S WORKING AT THE ORPHANAGE.
I'M SENDING YOU THERE.
...THE ORPHANAGE... LIEUTENANT PHERE MARSHEL...

RAIMON'S... WORKING?
Heh...
YOU'RE SURPRISED, TOO, PHERE?

COPY THAT.
DON'T HURT HIM.

I WOULD NORMALLY SEND INGRAM FOR A CHECKUP...
BUT HE'S TOO SWEET ON RAIMON.
SORRY ABOUT THAT.

WE DON'T WANT RAIMON STICKING HIS NOSE WHERE IT DOESN'T BELONG RIGHT NOW.
PHERE, YOU'RE IN CHARGE OF THE ORPHANAGE CASE, SO GO AND KEEP TABS ON HIM.

HE'S...
RAIMON IS...
...GOING TO BE MY RIGHT-HAND MAN.
I'LL...
...GET ON IT RIGHT AWAY...
...COLONEL.
ALL RIGHT.
THAT WAS THE LAST OF THE WASHING.

HM?
I-IT'S JUST A FIGURE OF SPEECH, YOU KNOW!!
KOTOBUKI?!
Oooh...
IT FEELS GOOD TO WAKE UP EARLY AND HANG THE WASHING.
ESPECIALLY WHEN YOU'RE BUMMED OUT.
YOU'RE BUMMED OUT?
WERE YOU ALL RIGHT YESTER-DAY?
WE WERE WORRIED ABOUT YOU.
NO PROBLEM. DID YOU SLEEP WELL?
IT'S KOTOBUKI!
KOTOBUKI!
Hey
DID YOU WASH YOUR FACE?
WE'VE BEEN TALKING...
ABOUT...?
WHAT COULD HAPPEN IF WE FOUND TSUBASA.

SOME PEOPLE BELIEVE IT'S STILL SOMEWHERE IN THE GROUND...
...AND THAT WHOEVER FINDS IT WILL HAVE HIS WISH GRANTED. IT'S A MYTH OF OUR TIME...
IF WE FOUND TSUBASA...
...WE'D ASK FOR OUR MOMS AND DADS.
TSUBASA...
I WANT TO PROTECT THIS ORPHANAGE.
GOT ANY PLANS?
AND THIS TIME...
...I'M NOT GOING TO JUST STAND THERE.
IT'S SAID THAT A LONG TIME AGO...
...TSUBASA SHOWED UP AND GRANTED EVERYONE'S WISHES BEFORE VANISHING.
But!!
YOU NEVER KNOW WHEN THEY'LL COME AT US.
It's better than just sitting around.
THAT'S NOT A PLAN, KOTOBUKI.
I'LL BE ON GUARD!

I'LL STAY WITH YOU, KOTOBUKI.
JUST DON'T DO ANYTHING ALONE, OKAY?
WOW. YOU COULD SEE HIM?
I REMEMBER THE FACE OF THE GUY WHO BROKE THE GLASS.
I'LL GET HIM AND MAKE HIM PAY FOR THE GLASS.
OF COURSE. I HAD TO TRAIN MY EYES WHEN I WAS A THIEF.
Oh!
"THEY'RE ALSO THE FIRST ONES TO COMMIT CRIMES."
I WONDER WHAT HE'S...
...UP TO NOW?
.....
...SURE.

I HOPE RAIMON'S KEEPING WATCH.
Dammit!
I WISH I COULD GET MY HANDS ON THEM..
ANYWAY...
...WHAT'S WRONG WITH THOSE BASHERS?
IF THEY WANT TO ATTACK THE ARMY, THEN JUST DO SO.
ボウ
チカッ
?
HE'S AT IT AGAIN...
WHERE'S HE GOING?
!!
"JUST DON'T DO ANYTHING ALONE, OKAY?"
BUT...
THIS COULD BE MY ONLY CHANCE!!
THAT'S THE BASTARD WHO BROKE THE GLASS!!

Yikes!
HE'S GOT FRIENDS.
ALL CLEAR. THEY'RE PRACTICALLY WAITING TO BE ATTACKED.
.....
HMM... WHAT SHOULD I DO...?
SO HOW WAS IT?
A HOUSE WITH ELECTRICITY, HUH?
THAT MANY PIG HOUSES?!
HOW MANY HAVE WE GOT?
LET'S FINISH THIS ONE OFF AND MOVE ON.
THOSE BASTARDS ...!!
NOW THAT'S WORK.
THIS ONE IS OUR FOURTH. SO...SEVEN MORE TO GO.

WHO ARE YOU?
ANSWER ME!!
THAT BITCH... IS WORKING IN THAT DUMP.
.....
SO YOU'RE THE ORPHANAGE BASHERS?!
THAT'S RIGHT.
THEY'RE OUR WORK.
WHAT ARE YOU GOING TO DO ABOUT IT?
I WON'T LET YOU DESTROY IT.
IF YOU HAVE ISSUES WITH THE ARMY, GO TO THEM!!

!!
SHUT UP!!
WE DON'T NORMALLY ROUGH UP GIRLS...
...BUT YOU'VE SEEN TOO MUCH.
AS A SEND-OFF GIFT, I'LL LET YOU IN ON THE TRUTH.
OUR GOAL ISN'T THE ARMY.
WE'RE BEING PAID TO DO THIS.
THE GUN I SAW IN TOWN...
.....

A PLAN?
WE'RE CLEANING OUT THE ORPHANAGES AS PART OF SOME "BIG PLAN."
AND THAT SUDDENLY MAKES IT OKAY?
WHO ARE WE TO SAY NO TO A LITTLE CLEAN UP IF WE GET PAID FOR IT?
WHAT KIND OF MAN WOULD WANT A NAMELESS ONE FOR A LOVER?
WHO CARES? IT'S JUST ANOTHER DUMP, GONE.
HE'D BE RIDICULED..
WE'RE DOING THOSE NAMELESS KIDS A BIG FAVOR.
...AND DISOWNED.
WHO WOULD WANT TO BE WITH A NAMELESS ONE?
A LOSER WHO DESERVES TO BE LAUGHED AT.
THINK ABOUT IT. THEY HAVE NO FUTURE. THEY'LL NEVER FIND A JOB, LET ALONE MARRY.

SO WHAT'S THE PLAN?
...ONCE WE'VE HAD SOME FUN.
SHE'LL BE SILENCED...
Heh...
RAIMON...
Oh.
GOOD IDEA.
WHA--
W-WAIT...
DESPIC-ABLE!
GET OFF...!
RAIMON...!

PHERE...
.....
WAY TO GREET A FORMER COLLEAGUE.
.....
WE'VE NOT SEEN EACH OTHER SINCE YOU LEFT THE ARMY...
...YET YOU RECOGNIZED ME INSTANTLY. GOOD FOR YOU.
THE WHIP WAS A DEAD GIVE-AWAY, PHERE.
I KNEW ROSS WOULD CONTACT YOU.
WHAT BUSINESS BROUGHT THE LIEUTENANT, NOT THE MAJOR, DOWN HERE?
ALL THE MORE REASON TO BELIEVE SOMETHING IS GOING ON.

I HAVE COME HERE BY ORDERS OF THE COLONEL.
THE ATTACKS?
OR THAT THING BEHIND ME?
FOR NOW.
I AM NOT HERE TO FIGHT.
YOU'VE STILL GOT...
...UNRESOLVED ISSUES WITH ME.

IT'S HIM AGAIN!!
AGAIN...
HOW DID HE GET IN?!
Th--
DON'T WORRY.
THESE BAD GUYS CAN'T DO ANYTHING TO YOU.
THANKS... UM...
WHO ARE YOU?
...?
THAT MAKES NO SENSE...
YOUR BOYFRIEND, RAIMON. DOES HE TREAT YOU WELL?
I KNOW YOU, KOTOBUKI.
YOU'RE THE PERSON WHO KEEPS THE PLANET GOING ROUND.
DO YOU LIKE HIM? IS HE SPECIAL TO YOU?
.....

THEN...
...YOU ARE HAPPY.
STOP ASKING...
...THE OBVIOUS.
BUT I'M NOT SURE ABOUT RAIMON.
MAYBE I'M MAKING HIS LIFE MISERABLE AND I DON'T KNOW IT...
...I AM.
WHY WOULD HE WANT A NAMELESS ONE FOR A LOVER?
"WHAT KIND OF MAN WOULD WANT A NAMELESS ONE AS A LOVER?"

MY...
ALL I WANT IS TO BECOME GOOD ENOUGH FOR RAIMON...
...BUT IF HE'S GOING TO BE RIDICULED BECAUSE OF ME...
...HEART WOULD BREAK.
SINCE THAT VERY COLD DAY...
...SINCE YOU WERE IN THAT ORPHANAGE.
WHY AM I OPENING UP TO A COMPLETE STRANGER?
YOU SHOULD BE MORE SELFISH...
...WHEN ANN LEEN TOOK YOU IN AS A BABY.
I KNOW YOU'VE BEEN TRYING SO HARD...

YOU'VE BEEN WORKING HARD EVER SINCE, HAVEN'T YOU?
.....
HOW...
...DO YOU KNOW ABOUT THAT?
...AND SO SAD...
ABOUT A PLACE SO SWEET AND SO WARM...

翼を持つ者

HOW DID YOU KNOW...?
ABOUT THE ORPHAN-AGE?
BUT...
HOW?
...BUT YOU WERE...
...VERY HAPPY THERE.
WHO IS HE?
YOU WERE VERY POOR WHEN YOU WERE IN THE ORPHANAGE...
I DON'T WANT RAIMON RIDICULED BECAUSE OF ME...
THAT WOULD BE TOO PAINFUL.

WE'RE HOME!
WE FOUND LOTS OF FIREWOOD.
ENOUGH TO KEEP US WARM THROUGHOUT THE WINTER!!
...YEAH.
Ah ha ha ha...
GOOD JOB, KOTOBUKI, TOTA!!

ANN TOOK ME IN AS A BABY.
SHE RAN A SMALL ORPHANAGE WITH FIVE OTHER NAMELESS KIDS.
THE ARMY GAVE US SOME MONEY...
...BUT NOT NEARLY ENOUGH TO LIVE ON.
WE REALLY STRUGGLED.
A BUD!!
WE'VE GOT BUDS!!
WOW!!
LET'S GIVE IT A YELL!
Good!
Hang in there!
I HAD EVERYONE I NEEDED.

...PARADING INTO THE TOWN.
Look.
THERE THEY GO AGAIN...
I'LL THROW STONES AT THEM IF THEY COME NEAR.
THEY'D BETTER STAY CLEAR.
I HAD...
...ANN.
STOP INSULTING ANN...!!
KOTOBUKI, TOTA...
STRAIGHTEN UP.
THAT LADY HAS A FAMILY NAME AND WAS FROM A DECENT BACKGROUND.
I DON'T KNOW WHY SHE BOTHERS.
SHE'S A HYPOCRITE. I DON'T WANT THEM NEAR US.

WHY SHOULD YOU FEEL ASHAMED OF BEING HUMAN?
I WANT YOU TO KEEP YOUR HEADS HELD HIGH!
LET'S DO IT.
THEY MAY CALL US NAMELESS ONES...
...BUT...
...WE ARE STILL HUMANS.
"PROOF OF LIFE." THOSE WERE HER FAVORITE WORDS.
SHE WAS SO STRONG AND PROUD.
LET'S FIND THE MEANING OF LIFE.
THE PROOF OF LIFE!

SWEET ANN...
YOU HAD THIS GOLD WATCH WHEN I FOUND YOU.
GOLD?

IT'S A VERY VALUABLE THING, KOTOBUKI.
YOUR PARENTS DIDN'T WANT TO GIVE YOU UP.
WHY?

WELL, FOR ONE THING, THEY WOULDN'T LEAVE SUCH A VALUABLE THING WITH YOU IF THEY DIDN'T CARE.
AND THEY COULD'VE LEFT YOU ON THE STREET, NOT IN FRONT OF OUR BUILDING.
.....
I DIDN'T HOLD A GRUDGE...
...BUT IT WAS HARD...

SINCE YOU ARE SIX, I WANT YOU TO KEEP IT.
TREAT IT WELL.
THEY DIDN'T HATE ME...
HOW-EVER...
...KNOWING THAT I HAD BEEN A BURDEN TO THEM.
PEOPLE IN TOWN WOULD LOOK AT US COLDLY...
...AND SAY WE WEREN'T WANTED.
BUT THE WATCH GAVE ME COURAGE.
IT'S FREEZING!!
IT'S YOUR MOM AND DAD'S PROOF OF LOVE!

IT WAS WARM...
...AND SWEET.
Yaaay!
HUDDLE UP!
MORE THAN ANYTHING, I HAD EVERYONE.
I HAD ANN.
WE'LL CURL UP TOGETHER. COME ON, KIDS!!
MY FAMILY...
TOTA?!
WHAT HAPPENED TO YOU?!

It's all right.
.....
IT WASN'T A RARE OCCURRENCE, BUT WE DIDN'T TELL ANN.
WE DIDN'T WANT TO MAKE HER SAD.
NOTHING.
THEY MUST'VE BEATEN HIM UP.
Dammit!!
STUPID GROWN-UPS, BEATING UP KIDS!!
YOU KNOW WHAT ANN ALWAYS TELLS US.
DON'T HOLD A GRUDGE. RISE ABOVE THEM.
YOU'RE RIGHT...
I'LL BE SOMEONE BIG...
...AND I'LL HELP MAKE LIFE EASIER FOR THE NAMELESS ONES.

THEN WILL YOU MARRY ME, KOTOBUKI?!
MARRY? WHAT'S THAT?
I'LL HELP THE NAMELESS ONES LIVE HAPPY LIVES.
AND WE'LL BE EVEN HAPPIER.
THAT'S MY PROOF OF LIFE...!
IT'S A PROMISE TO STAY TOGETHER FOREVER.
ANN AND EVERYONE CAN GET MARRIED, AND THEN WE'LL ALL HAVE A NAME.
WOW, TOTA...! I'LL WORK HARD AND BECOME BIG, TOO!
THEN I CAN PROTECT SOMEONE I LIKE!
WOW...

I DIDN'T WANT TO BE LEFT BEHIND ANYMORE.
I WON'T LET SOMEONE I CARE ABOUT BE RIDICULED!
LET'S FIND OUR PROOF OF LIFE.
LET'S DO IT.
BUT A FEW WEEKS LATER...
...ANN COLLAPSED.
Huff
Huff
...I'M FINE.
I JUST NEED TO REST.

ANN...
WHERE'RE YOU GOING, TOTA?
KOTOBUKI.
I'M THE FASTEST ONE. I'LL BE BACK IN A BIT!
I'LL GO!!
I'M GOING TO GET A DOCTOR. STAY WITH HER UNTIL I--
I HAVE TO TRY!!
SHE'S SUFFERING. SHE'S IN LOTS OF PAIN.
SHE MUST'VE GOTTEN SOMETHING FROM YOU NAMELESS ONES.
PLEASE COME AND SEE HER!!
I HAVE-TO DO IT NOW.
ANN IS ILL?
I HAVE TO PROTECT SOMEONE I LOVE!!

ドキッ!
MONEY...
SO WHAT? YOU HAVE NO MONEY!!
IT MUST BE THE EPIDEMIC COLD...
I DON'T HAVE ANYTHING FOR YOU NAMELESS ONES.
"YOUR PARENTS" PROOF OF LIFE...
ANN'S NOT NAMELESS!!
PLEASE...!!
BUT ...!!
ANN'S MY FAMILY...!!
SO GIVE ME MEDICINE!!
LOOK, THIS IS "GOLD" AND IT'S "VALUABLE." I'LL GIVE THIS TO YOU.

HANG IN THERE, ANN!!
ハッハッ
ハッハッ
ハッハッ
I'M COMING SOON!!
HERE.
ポイ
……!
THANK YOU...!!
ハッハッ
WHAT'S THAT SMELL?
ハッハッ
ハッハッ
ハッハッ
WHAT'S THAT?
……?
ハッハッ
IT'S BRIGHT. IS IT DAWN ALREADY?
ハッハッ

HUFF
"WHY SHOULD YOU FEEL ASHAMED OF BEING HUMAN?"
HUFF
HUFF
"LET'S DO IT."
HUFF
"LET'S FIND THE MEANING OF LIFE."

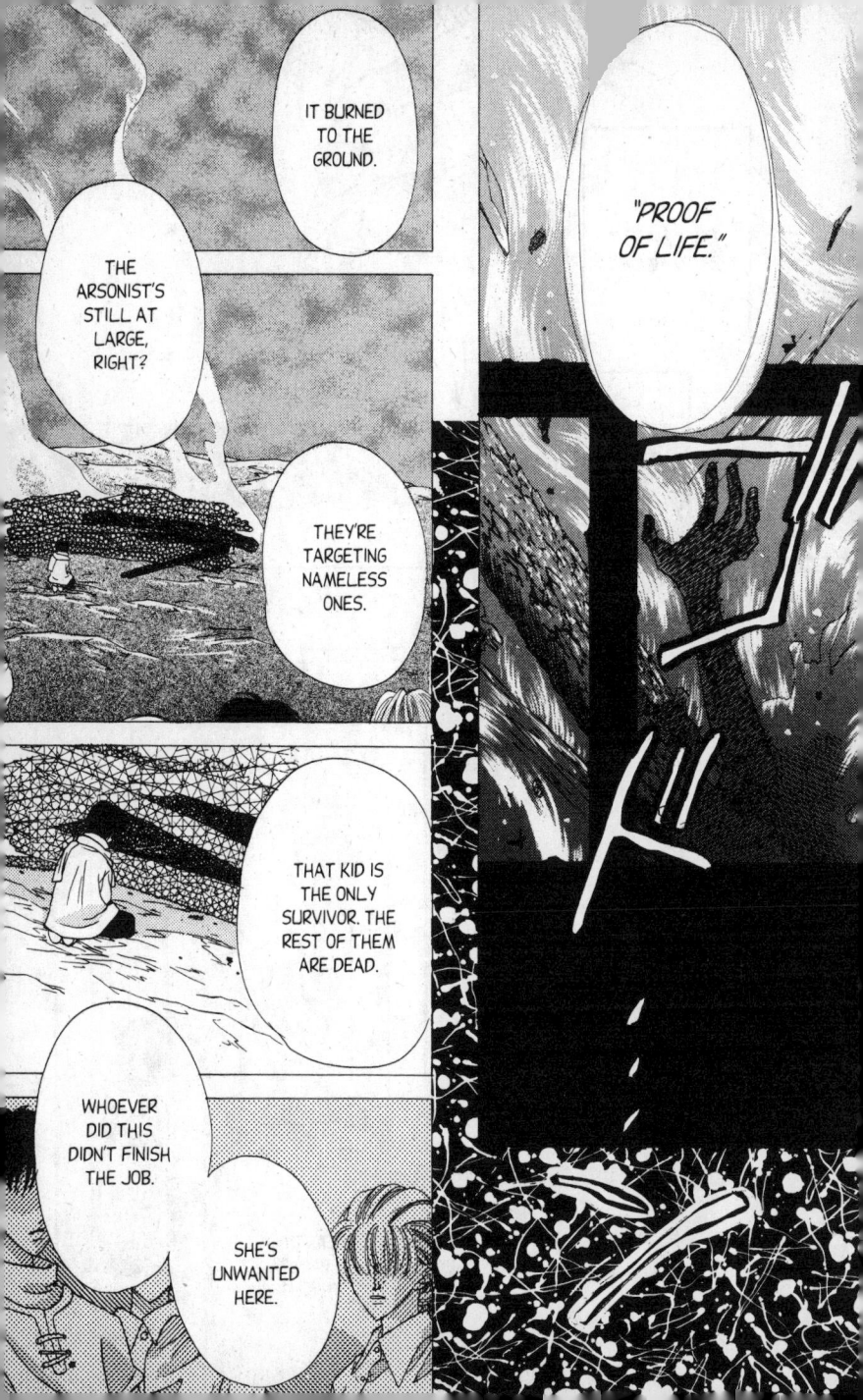
IT BURNED TO THE GROUND.
THE ARSONIST'S STILL AT LARGE, RIGHT?
THEY'RE TARGETING NAMELESS ONES.
THAT KID IS THE ONLY SURVIVOR. THE REST OF THEM ARE DEAD.
WHOEVER DID THIS DIDN'T FINISH THE JOB.
SHE'S UNWANTED HERE.
"PROOF OF LIFE."

SHE'LL START BLAMING US.
THEY HATED US SO MUCH...
...THEY WERE CAPABLE OF SUCH AN ATROCITY.
I WAS FALLING INTO PIECES.
SOMETHING LIKE THAT COULD HAPPEN AGAIN...
...THE SNEERS AND RIDICULE...
...THAT ANN HAD TO PUT UP WITH.
I'M FALLING APART.
I CAN'T PUT RAIMON THROUGH...
YOU REALLY CARE ABOUT RAIMON.

AFTER THE FIRE...
NO MONEY, NO JOB, NO NOTHING.
...I WAS LEFT ALL ALONE...
...SO I LEFT ON A JOURNEY.
I SOON FOUND MYSELF STEALING.

I KNEW IT WAS WRONG...
...BUT I HAD TO SURVIVE.
ALL I COULD THINK OF WAS HOW TO GET THROUGH EACH DAY.
AND...
"NICE TO MEET YOU. ARE YOU KOTOBUKI?"
"YOU'RE CUTE."
KOTOBUKI.
WHAT ARE YOU DOING HERE?
I SAW THE HOUSE GLOWING IN THE DISTANCE.

WHAT'S WRONG?
I FINALLY FOUND...
...MY PROOF OF LIFE.
IT'S RAIMON.
...I...
...WILL... WORK HARD...

I WON'T.
I'VE BUILT MY WORLD AROUND YOU, KOTOBUKI.
I WILL PROTECT SOMEONE I CARE ABOUT.
DON'T LEAVE MY SIDE...
I'LL BE GOOD ENOUGH FOR HIM.
I WON'T LET THEM TAKE HIM AWAY.
"IT'S A PROMISE TO STAY TOGETHER FOREVER."
I'M GOING TO MARRY YOU ONE DAY, KOTOBUKI.
ポン

"AND THEN WE'LL BE..."
"...EVEN HAPPIER."
UH-HUH...
ANYWAY...
WHY THE SUDDEN DOUBT?
MAYBE I NEED TO DEMONSTRATE MY LOVE MORE.
HUH?
WHAT?!
NOT NOW, NOT HERE, YOU IDIOT!!
BUT I WANT TO COMFORT YOU. ♡
N...
THAT'S NOT NECESSARY!! GET OFF!

DIDN'T YOU NOTICE...?
WE'RE NOT ALONE.
Oh?
Uh...
AND THEY SAID SOMEONE'S PAYING THEM TO DO IT!!
I SEE.
REALLY?
THEY'RE THE ORPHANAGE BASHERS!
I ALMOST FORGOT!!
YEAH. SOMEONE PUT THEM UP TO IT, RIGHT?
Hey!
ARE YOU LISTENING TO ME?!
I SAW THE BOY AGAIN.
AND...
WHO ARE YOU?
HOW DID YOU...

BANG
.....
RAI--
A BULLET PROOF JACKET
Phew...
YOU INTER-RUPTED US.
ANSWER MY QUESTION. YES OR NO.
IT WAS ROSS...
...WHO HIRED YOU, RIGHT?

GOOD ANSWER.
LET'S GO.
Huh?!
B-BUT...
WHAT?
.....YES
AND ROSS IS THE MASTERMIND OF THE ATTACKS?!
WHY ARE YOU FROZEN?
THIS GENTLEMAN NEEDS TO SEE A DOCTOR. HIS RIBS MAY BE PUNCTURING A LUNG.
Okay.
RIGHT?
ROSS IS RAIMON'S DAD, RIGHT?
Damn..!!
THAT SON OF A BITCH SHOT THE SAME PLACE FIVE TIMES!!
KA-CHAK

LOW COST AND CHEAP PRICE. IT GOES AROUND AND IS ILLEGAL.
Criminals.
ROSS'S COMPANY MANUFACTURES THIS GUN.
IT'S HIM.
BUT THAT DOESN'T MEAN ROSS IS INVOLVED...
Maybe his subordinates?
THEY ALL HAD THE SAME GUN.
DO YOU REALLY BELIEVE HIM? ABOUT YOUR FATHER BEING...
IT'S HIGHLY LIKELY.
HE'S A CRUEL BASTARD.
YOU'RE GOING TO DO HIM IN, RIGHT?
WHAT DID YOU MAKE IT FOR?!
And why?!
I INVENTED THIS CONVERTED GUN.
I'LL NEVER UNDERSTAND WHAT GOES THROUGH A GENIUS'S MIND!!
FOR FUN. ROSS STOLE IT FROM ME...
...a long time ago.

HIS OWN FLESH AND BLOOD.
IS HE REALLY CAPABLE OF...
...TURNING HIS BACK ON HIM?
...OR SUCH SADNESS.
...
WHAT HE DID TO THE ORPHANAGES WAS HORRIBLE.
NO ONE SHOULD HAVE TO GO THROUGH SUCH MISERY...
BUT...
IT'S HIS DAD.

That means...
...THAT RAIMON AND KOTOBUKI FOUND OUT. THAT'S PROBLEMATIC.
OKAY, GO TO HOSPITAL AND DON'T COME BACK FOR A WHILE.
klik☆
OH, DEAR.
I CAN'T WAIT.
IT LOOKS LIKE...
...WE'RE IN FOR A LITTLE BATTLE, LIEUTENANT MARSHEL.
ARE YOU UP FOR IT? THIS COULD BE A CHANCE FOR YOU TO BRING RAIMON DOWN.

ARE YOU READY, KOTOBUKI?
STOP IT.
DO I REALLY HAVE TO DO THIS?
YOU SHUT UP, OLD WOMAN.
I MEANT FOR YOU TO.
SHUT UP. STOP WHINING AND JUST DO IT.
Eh?!
I CAN HEAR YOU, YOU LITTLE BRAT!!
GET ON WITH IT. WE DON'T HAVE ALL DAY.
HERE, HOLD THIS.
WHAT'S THIS?
IT'S A MAKESHIFT MIKE.
IT'S NOT MY FAULT!
YOU DIDN'T EVEN BRING A MIKE...?
Useless woman.
KOTOBUKI ...
IT'S ROLLING.
YOU WERE SUPPOSED TO GIVE ME A HEADS-UP!!
ERM... UM!!
WHAT?!!!

Hi... Long time no see.
HOW'S IT GOING, GUYS? I'M DOING OKAY.
AND I LOOK A LITTLE DIFFERENT, DON'T I?!
YEAH, BUT IT'S BEEN EIGHT YEARS AND I'M A BIT NERVOUS.
EASY, KOTOBUKI. NO RUSH.
THANKS FOR PICKING UP *TSUBASA: THOSE WITH WINGS*!!
THAT'S IRRELEVANT.
DON'T WORRY. YOU LOOK PRETTY.
UH... I'M NOT MAKING MUCH SENSE.
IT'S JUST THE ART-WORK...
I HAVEN'T CHANGED INSIDE.
HEY!! YOU'RE TOO CLOSE!!!
IT'S FINE. YOU'RE SO PRETTY.
YOU'RE GOING TO BREAK THE "MIKE"!!

GAAAAH... STUPID LOVEBIRDS
YOU THINK THIS IS A BIG JOKE? THEY'LL THINK WE'VE GOT NO CLASS BECAUSE OF YOU TWO!!
WHOA ...
BUT IT'S TRUE...
Naturally...
AND YOU, RAIMON...
YOU'RE CUTTING ME OFF!!
RAIMON, GIVE ME THE CAMERA!! STOP TAPING ONLY KOTOBUKI.
YOU WANT TO DO IT, RIGHT?
IT WAS STUPID TO HAVE YOU DO THIS JUST BECAUSE YOU'RE THE MAIN CHARACTER!!
FORGET IT!! I'LL TAKE CARE OF THE REST!!

YOU KICKED HER!!
BOSS... WE SHOULD RUN.
STOP IT, RAIMON!!
BOSS, RUN... WATCH OUT, IT'S A CLIFF!!
ゴトッ
DON'T WORRY, THIS IS NOTHING STRANGE.
I HOPE YOU WON'T GIVE UP ON US. SEE YOU IN THE SECOND VOLUME!
...AHHHH!!!
カッ

Thank you.

Nice to meet you and hello!
It's been a while since I've worked on Tsubasa: Those With Wings. It feels a bit awkward to look at my earlier work. I still receive letters from Tsubasa fans. Thanks so much for your support! I wrote this series a long time ago and I know it's not perfect. I hope you come away with something good after you read this.

Natsuki Takaya

In Volume 2 of

Kotobuki has finally landed her dream job at the orphanage but nothing is ever that easy for her. Someone is trying to get the orphange closed down and Kotobuki will do whatever it takes to prevent it. But she faces a tough choice when it turns out that Raimon's father may be behind it all.

Coming in December 2008

Phantom Dream™

GENEIMUSOU by Natsuki Takaya
© Natsuki Takaya 1994

TAMAKI-CHAAN.
TAMAKI-CHAAAN!

BONK
SHUT UP, YOU IDIOT GIRL!!
OH.
TODAY I HAD TO WAKE UP AT FIVE AND WORK AGAIN, SO I'M SLEEPY.
DON'T IRRITATE ME ANYMORE THAN I ALREADY AM.
ASAHI.
TAA-MAAKII--
--CHAAN!
WHAAT KIND OF NONSENSE ARE YOU SPEWING THIS TIME, MY IDIOT OF A SON?
どさ
MOTH-ER ...
DON'T COMPLAIN BECAUSE I MADE YOU WAIT FOR ME--BE GRATEFUL!!
IT'S BECAUSE YOU KEPT ME WAITING FOR 20 WHOLE MINUTES, TAMAKI-CHAN.
How mean!
And do something about those huge eyes of yours!!

TAMAKI-CHAN, WHO'S ALWAYS IN A WORSE MOOD THAN USUAL IN THE MORNING, IS THE SOLE HEIR TO THIS TEMPLE...
...AND HE'S ALSO THE HEAD PRIEST.
AND THEN...
OH NO.
THEY'RE UP THERE CRYING BECAUSE THEIR WIFE/ DAUGHTER-IN-LAW GOT SO CRASS.
REALLY, HOW AM I GOING TO EXPLAIN TO YOUR GRANDPA AND FATHER UP IN HEAVEN THAT YOU GREW UP SO VIOLENT?
CRINKLE
YOU JUST DON'T WANT TO COOK!!
WHA--EEK!
FLAP
YOU ARE SO NOT CUTE. YOU'RE ABOUT TO LOSE YOUR DINNER, YOU KNOW.
!...
NOT REALLY.
DOESN'T THAT SEEM STRIKING TO YOU, TAMAKI?
THE WEAPON HAS NOT BEEN LOCATED, AND THE VICTIM SUFFERED MULTIPLE INJURIES THAT SEEM LIKE GOUGES...
IT SAYS THERE'S BEEN A BIZARRE INCIDENT AT TODA HIGH SCHOOL...
TODA HIGH...?
Where's that?

HAS NOTHING TO DO WITH ME.
OH, WAIT. WAIT!
WE'RE GOING NOW, MOTHER!
OKAY. BE CAREFUL NOW.
.....
AND THEN ...
WHEN IS THAT IDIOT SON OF MINE...
... GOING TO BECOME SELF-AWARE, I WONDER.
THE SOLE...
...HEIR.
REALLY, I'M SO SLEEPY.
THANK YOU FOR YOUR HARD WORK EVERY MORNING. ♡
.....
SORRY I HIT YOU.
It feels like I say this all the time, but...

TAMAKI-CHAN IS IMPORTANT TO ME.
WHEN WE GET TO SCHOOL, COULD YOU PLEASE SHOW ME YOUR PHYSICS HOMEWORK? PLEASE?
AT MY HOUSE, MY FATHER IS DEAD AND MY MOTHER WON'T STAY HOME WITH ME AT ALL, BUT...
DON'T YOU EVER FEEL LIKE DOING IT YOURSELF?
YEP, BUT I CAN'T DO IT.
It'd take the rest of my life, you know?
...I'M FINE AS LONG AS TAMAKI-CHAN'S THERE FOR ME.
ASAHI...
OTOYA-KUN HIT YOU AGAIN, DIDN'T HE?
What?!!
HOW'D YOU KNOW, JUN-CHAN?!!
THERE'S A BANDAGE ON YOUR HEAD.
Doh.
HE'S SO SCARY.
I CAN'T BELIEVE YOU CAN ACT NORMAL AROUND HIM.
HE'S KIND...
...AND STRONG, YOU KNOW.
TAMAKI-CHAN.

YOU'RE SO FAR GONE, YOU'RE SICK, ASAHI.
HERE.
COME IN.
HEY, HOMEROOM'S STARTING, YOU KNOW.
FIRST OFF, I'LL INTRODUCE THE TRANSFER STUDENT.
THIS IS MITSURU TORII.
SHE'S FROM TODA HIGH SCHOOL.
MITSURU-CHAN?!

MITSURU-CHAN!!
SIT.
Yes!
DID YOU HEAR?! DID YOU REALLY HEAR?! DO YOU REMEMBER?!
のしっ
IT'S MITSURU-CHAN, YOU KNOW, TAMAKI-CHAN.
URF.
I GET IT ALREADY, SO...
HUH? HUH?!
SHE WAS IN OUR NEIGHBORHOOD IN ELEMENTARY SCHOOL AND WE USED TO PLAY A LOT, HUH?
DOESN'T THAT SEEM STRIKING TO YOU...
...TAMAKI?
キーン
コーン
カ
DOOONG
DIIING

ガッ
TORII-SAAAN.
MITSU...
HEY, HEY. YOUR HAIR'S LONG, ISN'T IT? IT'S SO PRETTY.

OH...
TORII-SAN?
WHA...? UMM...

MITSURU-CHAN!!
ASAHI!
!?
!
ASAHI!

IT'S ME, ASAHI!
WHEN WE WERE IN ELEMENTARY SCHOOL WE PLAYED TOGETHER A LOT WITH TAMAKI-CHAN, REMEMBER?
I TOOK THE STAIRS TWO AT A TIME AND THOUGHT I'D TRIP!
gasp
gasp
gasp
THEY'RE FAST, FAST!-- THAT IS, YOUR LEGS ARE, MITSURU-CHAN!!
UMM...?
YOU'RE HINA, AREN'T YOU?!!
Wow!
MITSURU-CHAN, THAT'S THE NICKNAME YOU GAVE ME!
...!
I WANTED TO SEE YOU SO BAD!
YOU'RE SO TALL NOW!
giggle
YOU'RE STILL THE SAME HINA, AREN'T YOU...
MITSURU-CHAN, MITSURU-CHAAN.

SHOVE
GET BACK!!
EEK?!
WOBBLE
WHOA!
WHOA...
WHOA!
PLODF
YOU'RE REALLY HINA, AREN'T YOU?
MREOW?
THAT'S DANGEROUS, YOU KNOW.
What are you going to do if she turns into more of an idiot?
MITS--

NO...
DON'T COME OUT.
THIS OMINOUS PRESENCE IS...
MITSURU-CHAN?
NO. PLEASE.
SLIDE
THIS IS...
DON'T YOU DARE LAY A HAND ON EITHER OF THEM!!

AN EVIL SPIRIT!
TAMAKI-CHAN?!
THEY SAW!!
.....!!

.....
MITSURU-CHAN!!
!!
TAMAKI-CHAN.
YOU ALWAYS HAVE...
...YOUR JUZU, DON'T YOU?
*Note: Juzu are Japanese prayer beads.
TAMAKI-CHAN...
...HAS THE POWERS THAT THE CHILDREN OF THE OTOYA FAMILY INHERIT.
THAT'S RIGHT.

EVIL SPIRITS ...?
ASAHI-CHAN, YOU DON'T KNOW WHY SHUGOSHI EXIST, DO YOU?
IT'S TO EXORCISE EVIL SPIRITS.
THE SHIELD OF PROTECTION, THE CREATION OF SPIRIT SERVANTS, THE SUMMONING OF PROTECTIVE SPELLS...
A SHUGOSHI MANIPULATES THOSE PROTECTIVE TECHNIQUES.
THEY ARE THAT WHICH LATCH ON TO THE NEGATIVE FEELINGS IN YOUR HEART, LIKE SUSPICION AND HATRED...
...AND ACQUIRE STRANGE POWERS.
YOU SAW ONE WITH YOUR OWN EYES DIDN'T YOU?
IT'S HARD TO TELL UNTIL YOU ACTUALLY CATCH THEM, THOUGH.
TAMAKI-CHAN IS THAT SOLE HEIR.

YOU'D ALREADY SENSED IT? MOTHER...
I AM A BRIDE OF THE OTOYA FAMILY, YOU KNOW. OF COURSE I HAVE A BIT OF POWER.
TAMAKI.
ONCE AN EVIL SPIRIT IS BORN, YOUR BLOOD ATTRACTS IT, YOU KNOW.
IT DOESN'T MATTER THAT YOU DON'T LIKE IT.
I DEFINITELY SAW IT.
THE OTHER SHADOW THAT APPEARED BEHIND MITSURU-CHAN.
THAT'S AN EVIL SPIRIT?
WHY?!
...I DON'T KNOW.
I DON'T KNOW, AND IT HAS NOTHING TO DO WITH ME.

DING
DONG
LUNCH! LUNCH! LUNCH-TIME!
ASAHI, YOU'RE GOING WITH OTOYA-KUN AGAIN, RIGHT?
YEP.
TORII-SAAN!!
DO YOU WANT TO JOIN US? IT MUST BE BORING BY YOURSELF ALL THE TIME.
BA-DUM
DON'T BOTHER ME.
NEVER AGAIN.
I WON'T LET ANYONE GET CLOSE AGAIN.
I CAN'T GO BACK.

HEY...
YEP.
SHE'S COLD...
IT'S HARD TO GET CLOSE TO TORII-SAN, ISN'T IT...?
.....
I DIDN'T WANT TO SEE HER LIKE THIS.
I DID WISH I COULD SEE HER, BUT...
THE PERSON I THOUGHT OF LIKE A MOTHER...

BACK THEN, THE ONLY REASON I SMILED WAS BECAUSE TAMAKI-CHAN...
...AND MITSURU-CHAN WERE THERE.
...IN THE BAMBOO GROVE AT TAMAKI-CHAN'S HOUSE...
THE THREE OF US ALWAYS PLAYED TOGETHER...
HINA.
COME HERE, HINA.
I LOVE YOU, MITSURU-CHAN.
I CAN NEVER WIN WITH YOU.
I LOVE-LOVE TAMAKI-CHAN!
TAMAKI'S THE ONE YOU LOVE, RIGHT?
I LIKE-LOVE YOU, MITSURU-CHAN.
AFTER ALL, YOU'RE REALLY A KID.

YOU'RE STILL THE SAME HINA, AREN'T YOU...
MITSU-RU...
YOU'RE THINKING ABOUT HER, AREN'T YOU?
MITSURU-CHAN'S THE ONE WHO'S SCARED, YOU KNOW.
SHE'S THE ONE WHO'S SCARED THE MOST.
BE-CAUSE...

TA--
.....
Please stand by for a moment...
TAMAKI-CHAN? IT'S NOT LIKE I WANT A KISS RIGHT NOW, BUT--OH, IT'S NOT LIKE I DON'T NEED ONE EITHER, BUT...
IT'S JUST A REFLEX, BECAUSE YOU PUT YOUR FACE CLOSE TO MINE.
What the--?!
WHAT DID YOU SAY JUST NOW?! THEN ARE YOU SAYING THAT IF ANOTHER GIRL GETS THIS CLOSE TO YOU, YOU'D KISS HER, TOO?!
YOU'RE SAYING YOU WOULD EVEN IF IT WASN'T ME?! YOU'D DO IT TO SOME OTHER-- SOME OTHER GIRL ON THE STREET?!
...I GUESS YOU'RE A WOMAN, TOO.
YOU MEAN IT WOULD HAVE BEEN BETTER IF I WERE A BOY?!
How meeaan!

TAMAKI-CHAN?!
WHAT'S WRONG, TAMAKI-CHAN?!!
MITSURU?!
GET AHOLD OF YOUR-SELF.
PLEASE GET AHOLD OF YOURSELF.
THERE'S NO REASON I COULDN'T USE IT NOW.
RIGHT NOW, IF I USE THE SPELL...
BUT...
...EVEN IF I COULD USE IT...

EVERY-ONE'S LEGS ARE--!!
OW...
MY LEG...
WHAT'S WRONG, MANAGER?
HOW DID THIS...
ピーポー ピーポー
REE-000 REE-000 REE-000
ザワ
It's creepy, isn't it? Weird.
They said something might be wrong with their bones...
I have no clue, what's going on.
ARE THEY GOING TO BE ALL RIGHT...
THE TRACK TEAM...?
……
I DON'T SENSE THAT PRESENCE...
SHE'S NOT HERE ANY-MORE, IS SHE?
ザワ
……!
YOU'RE WRONG.
I BELIEVE--
I BELIEVE IN MITSU-RU-CHAN!
PLEASE BELIEVE IN HER...

YEAH...
I UNDER-STAND.
.....!
I FORGET MYSELF...
...MORE AND MORE...
giggle
MITSURU-CHAN.

I DON'T KNOW WHICH ONE IS ME...
I CAN'T ESCAPE.
...BUT...
MITSURU-CHAN?
.....!
!
IN ALL OF IT.
YOU'RE INVOLVED, AREN'T YOU?

...THAT'S RIGHT.
AFTER ALL, I CAN'T SAY NO.
SINCE IT'S MY FAULT.
NONE OF THIS WOULD HAVE HAPPENED IF I DIDN'T EXIST.
WHY...?
I LOVE YOU.
I REALLY LOVE YOU, MITSURU-CHAN!
IS THAT SO?
I HATE YOU.

ASAHI!
ASAHI!!
YOU'RE WRONG.
...MITSURU-CHAN WAS SMILING THE FIRST DAY SHE TRANSFERRED HERE!
THAT...
SHE REMINISCED AND CALLED ME "HINA"!

I BELIEVE IN THAT MITSU-RU-CHAN!!
WHAT A HAPPY-GO-LUCKY KID.
I COM-MEND YOU.
HA.
I WON'T FORGIVE...
BUT IT'S NO GOOD.
.....
WHO'RE YOU?
...THAT MITSURU...
...BECAUSE SHE TORTURED ME, WHO COULDN'T MOVE, THE WHOLE TIME.
MITSURU SINNED.

WHEN I COULDN'T EVEN RAISE MY HAND AND WAS STUCK IN A SICKBED, SHE WAS RUNNING AROUND LAUGHING.
WHO DOES SHE THINK SHE OWES THAT TO?
IT'S ALL BECAUSE I GAVE HER EVERYTHING, ISN'T IT?
I AM MINORU.
MITSURU'S YOUNGER TWIN SISTER.

STOP!

This is the back of the book. You wouldn't want to spoil a great ending!

This book is printed "manga-style," in the authentic Japanese right-to-left format. Since none of the artwork has been flipped or altered, readers get to experience the story just as the creator intended. You've been asking for it, so TOKYOPOP® delivered: authentic, hot-off-the-press, and far more fun!

DIRECTIONS

If this is your first time reading manga-style, here's a quick guide to help you understand how it works.

It's easy... just start in the top right panel and follow the numbers. Have fun, and look for more 100% authentic manga from TOKYOPOP®!